After Chapters & Verses

After Chapters & Verses

Engaging the Bible in the Coming Generations

Christopher R. Smith

Biblica Publishing
We welcome your questions and comments.

USA   1820 Jet Stream Drive, Colorado Springs, CO 80921
          ww.authenticbooks.com
India   Logos Bhavan, Medchal Road, Jeedimetla Village, Secunderabad
          500 055, A.P.

After Chapters & Verses

ISBN-13: 978-1-60657-044-9

12 11 10 / 6 5 4 3 2 1

Published in 2010 by Biblica

A catalog record for this book is available through the Library of Congress.

Printed in the United States of America

Contents

Introduction

The Time for Chapters & Verses Is Over

"By 2040 the Bible will be a 'thing of the past' for most people who claim to be Christ-followers," the Center for Bible Engagement warns, "if current trends of Biblical illiteracy continue."[1] Other researchers echo this prediction. David Kinnaman of the Barna Group reports that the younger a person is, the less likely they are to read the Scriptures.[2] An earlier Gallup poll showed the same trend.[3] Young Americans are walking away from the Bible.

Why? One primary reason[4] is that the Bible, as we present it and use it today, bears the strong imprint of modernity. The farther we move into postmodernity, the more difficult it will be for people to access this modern cultural artifact. Eventually, it will become almost impossible.

One of my most important premises in this book will be that postmodernity involves a change in our strategy for knowing. Postmodernity is difficult to define precisely, because it hasn't fully emerged. We can't yet describe everything it's going to be. We're still trying to distinguish

the aspects of our present culture that truly represent the
advent of postmodernity from those aspects that represent
late or hyper-modernity instead. As Stephen Joel Garver,
a professor of philosophy at LaSalle University, observes,
"postmodern" is

> a complex phenomenon. For instance, we can
> distinguish between postmodern*ism* as a theo-
> retical critique of philosophical modernism and
> postmodern*ity* as a cultural condition. We can also
> distinguish between aspects of the postmodern that
> are, in fact, hyper-modern—the modern come to
> its fullest and most self-conscious expression—and
> aspects of the postmodern that represent a genuine
> critique of and counter-practice to modernity.[5]

In other words, some of what we call postmodernity may
actually be hyper-modernity or counter-modernity. Right
now it's hard to tell the difference. But I do believe that we
can at least say, at this point in our cultural transition, that
in postmodernity the context of knowledge changes from
what it was in modernity. To state the matter very simply,
for modern people, truth came from facts and reason. For
postmodern people, truth is accessed through personal
experience and expression. For them, truth is less abstract
and certain and stateable. It's more practical, personal,
tentative, and impressionistic. But this doesn't mean there
isn't any truth for postmodern people. (I believe that's a
hyper-modern premise instead.) In postmodernity, truth is
just found, experienced, and held in a different way than it
was in modernity.

Donald Miller shares an experience that showed him how postmodern young adults, given their different approach to knowing, can't engage the Scriptures any more in the modern way we've been presenting them.

I had a conversation with my friend Omar, who is a student at a local college. For his humanities class, Omar was assigned to read the majority of the Bible. He asked to meet with me for coffee, and when we sat down he put a Bible on the table as well as a pamphlet containing . . . five or six ideas [that summarized "the gospel"]. He opened the pamphlet, read the ideas, and asked if these concepts were important to the central message of Christianity. I told Omar that they were critical; that, basically, this was the gospel of Jesus, the backbone of Christian faith. Omar then opened his Bible and asked, "If these ideas are so important, why aren't they in this book?"

"But the Scripture references are right here," I said curiously, showing Omar that the verses were printed next to each idea.

"I see that," he said. "But in the Bible they aren't concise like they are in this pamphlet. They are spread out all over the book."

"But this pamphlet is a summation of the ideas," I clarified.

"Right," Omar continued, "but it seems like, if these ideas are that critical, God would have taken the time to make bullet points out of them. Instead, He put some of them here and some of

them there. And half the time, when Jesus is talking, He is speaking entirely in parables. It is hard
to believe that whatever it is He is talking about can
be summed up this simply."

Omar's point is well taken. And while the ideas
presented in these pamphlets are certainly true, it
struck me how simply we had begun to explain the
ideas, not only how simply, but how nonrelationally,
how propositionally.[6]

Omar was assigned to read the Bible because his college
considered it an important cultural document. But he
couldn't connect the literature he was reading in it with
the interpretive framework he was being offered by people
who saw the Bible as something more—as the authoritative guide to life and faith. The frustration he expressed
suggested he was unlikely to keep reading the Bible when
it was no longer required as a class assignment.

Omar got frustrated when his postmodern sensibilities
balked at the modernistic isolation and systematization of
information in the pamphlet he was given. He recognized
that the meaningful units in the Bible were the literary
creations within it (such as the parables of Jesus). As a
postmodern person, he needed to work with the text in all
of its intricate literary development. That was the way he
would meet the God that the Scriptures, throughout their
length and breadth, are always seeking to introduce us to.
This wasn't going to happen for him through propositions
derived or distilled from the text. He didn't need the Bible
to be turned into "bullet points."

There are many Omars out there already, and their number is growing every day. For their sake, we need to rethink our modern approaches. We need to reflect the literary character of the Bible in our presentations and practices—in the way we publish the text, and in the way we read, study, preach, and teach it. This will enable postmodern young people to reconnect with the Bible. It will also help people who are already reading it experience a fresh new encounter with the Scriptures.

In other words, there's really no reason to despair. Anyone who cherishes the Bible as the word of God and knows of its life-transforming power should be deeply concerned about the precipitous decline we're witnessing in Bible reading in younger generations. But this concern should make us ask, seriously and sincerely, whether something needs to change in the way we've been presenting and using the Scriptures. Asking this question will make us open to an insight that can lead to new approaches that will ultimately reverse the decline: there's a difference between *what the Bible is* and *how it has been shaped in a given cultural context.*

Any cultural context other than the one in which the Scriptures were first created will not be able to recapture them perfectly in their original form.[7] But some contexts will be more hospitable to this form, while others will recast the Bible more significantly, as modernity has done. As we move into postmodernity, the challenge for us is to remove the modern imprint and return the Bible, through new presentations and practices, to something much closer to what it actually is. This will make the Scriptures more accessible to postmodern people.

The Bible, in its most essential form, is a *collection of literary creations.* These are its meaningful units. Stories, songs, poems, letters, and dreams naturally fill its pages. These are perfect vehicles for communicating spiritual understanding to the people of a postmodern culture that conceives of truth as nonpropositional, narrative, and experiential.

But isn't it already clear that the literary creations in the Bible are its essential units? Not really. The treasury of divinely inspired, spiritually transforming literature has always been there beneath the surface. But through changes over time in the Bible's presentation and uses, that surface has become hard and opaque. As Richard Moulton has observed,

> We are all agreed to speak of the Bible as a supremely great literature. Yet, when we open our ordinary versions, we look in vain for the lyrics, epics, dramas, essays, sonnets, treatises, which make the other great literatures of the world. Instead of these, the eye catches nothing but a monotonous uniformity of numbered sentences, more suggestive of an itemized legal instrument than of what we understand as literature.[8]

Moulton is saying, in other words, that the form of the Bible—the way it is now *presented)*—keeps us from recognizing and approaching the Scriptures as a collection of literary creations.

Our Bible *practices* can have the same effect. Brian McLaren describes "one of the ways to kill the Bible":

> You can read its ragged stories and ragamuffin poetry, and from them you can derive neat abstractions, sterile propositions, and sharp-edged principles. . . . You can sanitize the text of all evocative language, paradox, multiple perspectives, and interesting, three-dimensional people to end up with cute little morals, simple two-dimensional systems, and flat, boring prose that reads like a legal code or assembly instructions for a bicycle.[9]

In other words, through the way we use it, as well as through the way we present it, what the Bible really is can disappear behind what it appears to be.

How was the Bible put in its present form, and how did we come to use it as we do? Garver explains that "[w]hat we encounter as the Bible . . . is not what most Christians encountered as the Bible until the early modern era." In terms of the physical form of the Scriptures,

> with the advent of the moveable type printing press, the phenomenology of encounter with the sacred text shifted. The medieval encounter involved hand-written texts in multiple volumes and orders, primarily liturgical in use, heard more than read, and when read, often accompanied by the gloss. With the printed text, a single-volume Bible became a reality, with a standardized order, a fixed object of reading, placed under new forms of scrutiny.[10]

The medieval assortment of loose manuscripts was actually a much better visual clue to what the Bible is—a collection of literary compositions—than the single-volume printed presentation. This modern Bible looked instead like one of the encyclopedias that would be created as the great cultural project of the Enlightenment. And in modernity the Bible actually did come to be seen and used precisely as if it were an encyclopedia, a compendium of essential facts and propositions. The Bible began to send a strong visual signal that it should be approached this way when verse divisions were introduced in the mid-1550s and publishers began printing each "Bible verse" as a separate paragraph.

Modernity introduced another significant change to the presentation of the Scriptures. The order of the biblical books had been relatively fluid before the modern period, but with the advent of printing, it became fixed. This allowed people to gain quick access to materials anywhere in the Bible, independently of their context, using a "book, chapter, and verse" reference. Following these coordinates became the key to navigating through the Scriptures in the popular mind.[11] And so the Bible was recast to reflect two key values of modernity: information and speed.

But even though this grid had been superimposed on the Bible, it remained a literary collection. In its essence, it was still not an organized, encyclopedic compendium of useful and interesting information. Thus the modern reshaping of the Bible actually created a work that appeared to be, as Stanley Grenz and John Francke have put it, "a rather loose and disorganized collection of factual, propositional statements"[12] that needed to have some order imposed on it. Systematic theologians of the modern period rose to this organizational task enthusiastically. Eventually various interpretive systems were incorporated right into the biblical text, in the form of cross-references presented in a center column on the page—a modernistic gloss. These cross-reference systems portrayed the Scriptures as a soft-bodied creature that couldn't stand on its own and needed to be propped up from the outside by an exoskeleton. The visual message, confirmed by usage, was that the structure of the Scriptures was not to be found somewhere within the Bible itself, but outside it, in systems built around it. Its basic units of meaning were extracted propositions arranged in chains of references.

Even with the advent of postmodernity, our presentations, and the message they send about what the Bible is, haven't essentially departed from this modern form. Most Bibles, it should be acknowledged, are no longer printed with each verse as a separate paragraph. Instead, in a commendable effort to allow the literary character of the text to reassert itself against the chapter-and-verse overlay, most publishers now present the text in longer paragraphs that are intended to reflect more natural divisions. They even run these paragraphs right through chapter breaks when necessary. At the same time, however, modern publishers have left the chapter and verse numbers in place, prominent in the midst of the text. They've also introduced section breaks, with headings that conspicuously break up the flow of reading. These sections powerfully reassert the encyclopedic character of modernity's Bible. They continue to suggest that the Scriptures are a collection of short discussions on topics of interest. They still invite us to dip in here and there for information.

We should not underestimate the power that the present form of the Bible holds over our imaginations. We may even be able to *say* what the Bible really is, but still be unable to *see* it. At the start of a video promotion for a recently published edition of the Scriptures, the narrator says, "The Bible is an unparalleled collection of poetry, prose, history, law, prophecy, and letters."[13] But even as she speaks these words, a Bible appears on the screen with each verse printed as a separate paragraph. The text is set in two columns, with a narrow strip of cross-references down the center. This is actually not the format of the product being advertised. But the video needed a picture of "the Bible" to accompany its opening words, and so it presented this iconic image that modern Christians recognize and cherish. This image sends a very strong visual signal that the Bible is *not* an "unparalleled collection" of literary compositions. It's an indexed compendium of propositional statements.

Why do we "see" the Bible in this iconic form when we picture it in our minds? I'm convinced it's because the *form* of the Bible represents the *authority* of the Bible for many of us. Later in this book I'll describe how the International Bible Society (now Biblica) developed *The Books of The Bible,* an edition of the Scriptures that has no chapter or verse numbers or section headings. When one young man got a copy of *The Books of The Bible* and saw only the bare text of Scripture on the page, he wrote on his blog, "My very first impression was one of discomfort. It felt weird and somewhat disrespectful to me to pick up the Bible as a book without those little verse numbers and chapter headings. Bibles have those." (Another blogger wondered similarly, after seeing the edition himself, "Would a Bible be a Bible without the little numbers scattered across its pages?") After reading in this edition for a short time, however, the first blogger reported:

> Reading Scripture this way flows beautifully and so far I can say that rather than missing the verse numbers and chapter headings, I like them gone. They got in the way. They disrupted the story. Most importantly, I think, they have offered us a convenient way to divide and misquote scripture in ways they weren't intended. Novels aren't written this way, why should God's story be any different?

Through a new presentation, this young man came to have a new appreciation for the Bible. But in order to break through to this appreciation, he needed to get past what was essentially an authority issue: he felt it was "disrespect-ful" to remove the Bible's traditional garb.

The danger is that we may actually ascribe more authority to the shape the Bible has taken over time than to what the Bible really is. Why, for example, do congrega-tions typically expect preachers to provide chapter and verse references for the biblical statements they quote in their sermons? It may be so that people can look them up and verify them if they want, or it may be so that people can take notes. In my experience as a preacher and a listener, however, I've found that most people don't look up or write down these references. But they do give an approving nod when they hear them. Quoting by chapter and verse feels authoritative, rigorous, trustworthy. It suggests the preacher really knows the Scriptures. Referencing by context and content instead may actually indicate a greater knowledge of the Bible, but in many places today, referring to "what Jeremiah wrote in his letter to the exiles" rather than to "Jeremiah 29:11" would probably create the impression that a preacher couldn't quite place a biblical statement, and was therefore unreliable. One user of *The Books of The Bible* reported he was getting exactly this kind of response:

> In my own teaching, I've made a point for some time of trying to avoid giving chapter and verse . . . but instead referring to the point actually being made, the way a teacher in a literature class would cite a passage. In fact, I've gotten some negative feedback on this practice from people who felt that stating the content of a passage wasn't as "edifying" as quoting the line and giving its chapter-and-verse numbers.

Clearly, for many of us, it feels almost unholy to conceive of the Bible as something other than a book with chapters and verses. Our minds insist, "Bibles have those."

But they don't. At least, they haven't always had them. Michele Brown, who was the curator of an exhibit on "Bibles Before the Year 1000" at the Freer Gallery of Art, acknowledges that the Bible "now seems straight-forward and iconic . . . as if it's always been there as just one thing." However, she explains, as different cultures present and transmit the Scriptures over time, actually "it's our perception that changes, and that helps to bring the idea of an iconic thing like 'the Bible' into creation."[14] In other words, we have come to take certain presentations and practices for granted, believing they truly represent *what the Bible is.* But in reality they largely reflect instead *what the Bible has become,* as we have shaped it in our own cultural image.

But isn't there some enduring value in the features that were added to the Bible in modernity? Yes. They can still help fulfill their original purpose, which was to allow scholarly reference works to be created. As we'll see in Chapter 1, chapters were added so that commentaries could be written, and verses were introduced so a concordance to the Greek New Testament could be compiled. Since then, chapters and verses, within a fixed book order in an entire Bible available in a single volume, have provided a convenient and standardized reference tool that has promoted extensive scholarly study in support of Scriptural understanding. If such a system didn't already exist, it would have to be invented. So the chapter and verse divisions we already have, particularly given their widespread and conventional acceptance, should not be dispensed with entirely.

Nevertheless, as we'll also see in Chapters 1 and 2, significant problems arise when we treat chapters and verses (and even some biblical "books") as *intentional units* within the text of Scripture. They're not reliable guides to the Bible's real form and meaning. But this is just how our current Bible practices treat them. We consider a chapter a week in Bible studies or sermons, as if chapters were meaningful, intentional units; we collect, memorize, display and quote "Bible verses" as if they were originally freestanding propositions that are meaningful outside a wider literary context. In other words, we have allowed the modern features of the Bible to shape our *devotional practices*. They've become centered around chapters and verses. In Chapters 4 through 7 of this book, I'll describe other approaches to reading, studying, preaching, and teaching that I feel are much more respectful of the Bible's actual character as a collection of literary creations. These new practices will allow us to keep our chapter-and-verse Bibles where they belong, on the reference shelf (next to our concordances, lexicons, and commentaries), and to use new presentations as our all-purpose Bibles for worship services, group studies, and private devotions.

I'll be using *The Books of The Bible* to illustrate the new approaches I'm advocating. In Chapter 3 I'll tell the story of how this edition was created. I believe it puts the Scriptures in a form that encourages people to develop the new approaches we should be cultivating for postmodernity. I hope and expect that many other versions of the Bible will be issued in similar formats. Each one will further our understanding of how new presentations can help people engage God's word more effectively. But I find that the practices that readers of *The Books of The Bible* have already been developing are worthy of our immediate consideration, since they point forward clearly to the new approaches we need to take.

Since the edition was published nearly three years ago, I've followed what users have been saying about it in articles, reviews, and blog posts, and on Facebook and in similar venues. I've corresponded with many of them, and they've described for me in more detail the new approaches the format is encouraging them to take. These exchanges have been fascinating and encouraging. They show that an exciting new era of Bible engagement is on the horizon. I'll be sharing many users' experiences in the pages ahead.

When I consider that entire generations are walking away from the Scriptures, and that our current presentations and practices, shaped in modernity, may be significantly responsible, I feel a great sense of urgency. The Bible is our sacred book, a gift to us from God. If it's been reshaped over time to the point where its essential character has been lost, we have every right to take it back. We don't need to be bound by the historical and cultural developments that have put it in its present form. "Sure, the chapters don't really line up with the material," we may say, "but they're convenient, and we're used to them." There's no room for this kind of complacency. There should be a revolt.

Actually, one is already under way. People are rebelling with their feet, as they walk away from the Bible. Only significant changes will bring them back. Those changes need to begin with presentations and practices that reclaim the literary creations within the Bible as its meaningful units. Then what God is saying to us through the Scriptures will once again be experienced as meaningful communication.

Chapter One
The Problem with Chapters & Verses

C hapters and verses, as I've just explained, were added to the Bible for a positive reason. Unfortunately, they've since become the most prominent features of a historical and cultural reshaping that has altered the meaning we'd otherwise find in the Bible. It has distorted the beauty of literary form and expression in the Scriptures. The more we learn about the history of chapters and verses, the more clearly we recognize that they aren't a natural or essential part of God's word to us.

The chapter and verse divisions we know today aren't the work of the biblical authors. They were introduced well over a thousand years after the last books of the Bible were written, and they're only the latest in a series of systems that have been used at various times to mark smaller portions within the biblical text.

The entire Old Testament except for Psalms was divided into paragraphs or *parashoth* even before the time of Christ.[1] For example, each of the "days of creation" at the beginning of Genesis was a single *parashah*. (By contrast, in our Bibles, these "days" consist of three to eight verses each.) The five books of Moses were also divided in a different way so they could be read out loud in the synagogue. In Palestine they were divided into 154 *sedarim* (weekly lessons) so they could be read over the course of three years. In Babylon, however, these books were read through every year, so they were divided into 54 parts there. Each of these parts was also called a *parashah,* even though they didn't correspond to the other divisions known by that name.[2]

The New Testament writings were divided early in their history into topical sections of varying lengths known as *kephalaia*. Matthew was divided into 68 *kephalaia*, Mark into 48, Luke into 83, and so forth. These divisions were probably introduced around the fourth century. But some manuscripts illustrate that different systems were used to divide the text even earlier; the *kephalaia* system was added to these manuscripts when it became the standard. The scholar and historian Eusebius introduced a different system of his own in the fourth century when he divided the gospels into parts that he listed in ten tables, or "canons." He assigned passages to various tables based on which gospels they were found in.[3]

Smaller portions within the Bible were marked in all these different ways long before the chapter and verse divisions we know today were ever introduced. But these marking systems weren't treated as an inherent part of the Bible. *Parashoth* and *sedarim* were indicated by single letters in the text. Most people only ever heard the Scriptures read out loud, so they weren't aware of them. The canons of Eusebius were marked by roman numerals in the margins.

Chapters were added to the Bible around the year 1200 by Stephen Langton. He was an English church leader who studied and taught at the University of Paris before becoming Archbishop of Canterbury. While in Paris, Langton wrote extensive biblical commentaries. He introduced chapter divisions to an edition of the Vulgate (the Latin Bible) so that he and others could cite passages more conveniently in their commentaries. Eventually these divisions were incorporated into manuscripts of the Hebrew Old Testament and the Greek New Testament, and later into printed Bibles. Even so, chapters weren't treated as an inherent part of the Scriptures at first. When Johannes Gutenberg created the first printed Bibles in the 1450s, he didn't print any chapter numbers. Illustrators had to add them in the margins.

The verse system we know today was introduced to the New Testament in 1551 by the French linguist, classical scholar, and printer Robert Estienne (also known as Stephanus). In his fourth edition of the Greek New Testament, he divided the text into verses because he wanted to produce a concordance. (This project was finally completed after his death by his son Henry in 1594). The Old Testament had already been divided into "verses" of a sort. By the early centuries of our era, those who read the Hebrew Scriptures aloud in the synagogues had to pause at regular intervals to allow for an Aramaic translation, since most Jews no longer spoke Hebrew. By the year 500, the short stretches of text that were read before a translation had become standardized. They were indicated in manuscripts by a *soph pasuq* mark (:).[4] Even so, two different systems remained in use, one in Palestine and the other in Babylonia, until they were harmonized by ben Asher in the tenth century. When Stephanus versified the New Testament over five hundred years later, similar "verses" were created in the Old Testament by numbering the stretches of text between *soph pasuq* marks in ascending order within each of the chapter divisions that Stephen Langton had introduced two hundred and fifty years before. It was at this point that chapters and verses began to be printed within the text.

Given this history, and particularly the great distance in space, time, and culture between the biblical authors and those who later added chapters and verses to their works, it's not at all appropriate to treat these additions as if they belonged in the text and marked intentional units. We shouldn't consider them reliable guides in our efforts to appreciate the Bible's form and meaning. Significant problems arise when we do.

"The Bible," a friend once said to me, "looks like a bad technical manual that you don't want to read." I knew what he meant. Chapter and verse numbers in the text of Scripture create the impression that the biblical authors were all writing the same kind of document—that for some reason, they were all composing their works a sentence at a time, numbering these sentences sequentially, and then gathering them into larger numbered groups. This impression is only heightened when each verse is printed as its own separate paragraph.

Chapters and verses thus keep us from recognizing the variety of literary forms in the Bible. This is a serious handicap to readers, because the different forms really should be read in different ways. As Gordon Fee and Douglas Stuart write in *How to Read the Bible for All Its Worth*,

> [T]o communicate His Word to all human conditions, God chose to use almost every available kind of communication: narrative history, genealogies, chronicles, laws of all kinds, poetry of all kinds, proverbs, prophetic oracles, riddles, drama, biographical sketches, parables, letters, sermons and apocalypses. To interpret properly the . . . biblical texts . . . one needs to learn the special rules that apply to each of these literary forms (genres). . . . [T]he way God communicates His Word to us in the "here and now" will often differ from one form to another.[5]

Unfortunately, however, because the Bible's various literary forms have basically been homogenized by chapter and verse numbering, we are instead susceptible to reading observations as if they were promises or commands, to thinking that figurative or symbolic language should be taken literally, and to making many other interpretive mistakes.

Most recent versions of the Bible strive to overcome this problem by using different formats to present the various Scriptural genres (kinds of writing) appropriately on the page. Narrative is printed as prose, but poetry is printed line-by-line, genealogy in columns, and so forth. Nevertheless, the chapter and verse numbers remain within the text, and they undercut the impression that the books of the Bible should be read as whole literary works of different genres.

A second problem with chapters and verses is that they typically don't follow a book's inherent divisions. That is, they not only disguise literary *genre*, they also distort literary *structure*. We'll first consider the significant ways that chapters do this, and note some of their other effects. We'll then see how verse divisions also fail to correspond with the biblical writers' units of thought, and how they create further problems of their own.

We don't need to look very far into the Bible to find badly placed chapter breaks. The very first chapter division in the Bible, in fact, between Genesis 1 and 2, breaks up a coherent unit, because it divides the seventh day of creation from the first six. This chapter break may be largely responsible for the way interpretation of this passage has come to focus on the "when" of creation, sparking debates about whether the "six days" are literal, twenty-four-hour periods. The "who" and "why" of creation are actually much more important concerns in Genesis. (If this chapter break had been placed at the end of the seventh day instead, it would have corresponded with the start of a natural unit within the book, the "generations of the heavens and the earth.")

Many other examples of badly placed chapter breaks could easily be given. The break between Romans 7 and

8, for instance, separates Paul's discussion of what it's like to live under the law—to know what God expects, but not have the power to do it—from the glorious solution to this problem he then proclaims in the gospel: "the law of the Spirit who gives life has set you free from the law of sin and death." Because "Romans 7" has now been isolated, as if it were an independent treatise, from the larger discussion it belongs to, the helpless condition it describes is often considered normative for believers. I don't think it is. But no matter how we understand Paul's comments in Romans 7, we shouldn't interpret them without reference to what he writes immediately afterward.

Badly placed chapter breaks also interfere with our understanding of many other passages that may be less well known. For example, in the book of Hebrews, the break between chapters 4 and 5 cuts off the beginning of the discussion of Jesus as high priest. It attaches it to the end of the preceding discussion, of Jesus as "apostle." The break between Malachi 3 and 4 cuts that book's closing oracle in half. (This break doesn't appear at all in the Hebrew text, where Malachi has only three chapters.) And the division between Nehemiah 6 and 7 splits off the end of a description of how the Jerusalem wall was completed and attaches it to a genealogy that follows.

Beyond noting individual examples like these from various parts of the Bible, we can also proceed more systematically to demonstrate how chapters typically don't correspond with the biblical books' inherent divisions. We can take up a book of the Bible, eliminate its chapter and verse divisions, and then trace the development of its argument or narrative. We can then go back and check where the chapter breaks were placed. In many cases, we'll discover they're highly disruptive.

For example, when we consider Colossians without chapters and verses, we find that it has three major sections. (1) Since Paul hasn't met the Colossians, he begins his letter to them by laying down some relational and doctrinal foundations. (2) In the main body of the epistle, he then presents correction, followed by instruction. (3) The letter ends, finally, with personal greetings. If, after this brief survey of its contents, we were asked to divide Colossians into four chapters of roughly equal length, we could easily identify how to create four internally coherent units of about the same size:

1. Relational and Doctrinal Foundations
2. Correction
3. Instruction
4. Personal Greetings

The chapter divisions themselves create four sections of roughly equal length within the book of Colossians, and the break between chapters 2 and 3 comes right where we might expect, between "correction" and "instruction." But this is the only well-placed chapter division in the book. To illustrate how bad the others are, let me provide a thematic outline of Colossians in a bit more detail, with the current chapter divisions marked by (x):

I. Relational and Doctrinal Foundations
    A. Paul's Prayer
    B. Paul's Gospel

    C. Paul's (x) Struggle
II. Correction and Instruction
    A. Correction: No Spiritual Status Symbols
    (x) **B.** Instruction
        1. Off with the old, on with the new
        2. Responsibilities of those in and under authority
            a. Wives and husbands
            b. Children and parents
            c. Servants (x) and masters
        3. Attitude toward outsiders/opponents
    III. Concluding Greetings

The break between chapters 1 and 2 actually cuts off a small part of the opening "foundations" section, grouping it with "correction." Even worse, it doesn't even preserve the smaller units within this opening section, where Paul shares first his prayer, then his gospel, then his struggle. Instead, this chapter break divides "Paul's struggle" into two parts, and groups the second with the "correction" that follows, even though a very clear transitional statement intervenes: "So then, just as you received Christ Jesus as Lord, continue to live your lives in him." How are readers to make sense either of chapter 1, which has an important piece missing at the end, or of chapter 2, which begins misleadingly with the ending of a previous section? This is the equivalent of interrupting the last movement of Bach's First Brandenburg Concerto in the middle, and then, after a pause, playing the rest of this movement and continuing without a break into the first movement of the Second Concerto. It's artistically absurd.

But the worst division of all is between chapters 3 and 4. It comes in the *middle* of II.B.2.c. That is, it actually breaks up a sub-sub-subsection. Dividing just one sentence later would have kept this unit together ("servants and masters") and also the larger discussion it's part of ("responsibilities of those in and under authority"). And placing the division only a little bit farther into the book would have resulted in a very logical placement, at the end of II and the beginning of III.

So why was this chapter division put where it was? No doubt the desire was to emphasize the command, "Masters, provide your slaves with what is right and fair." But the true meaning and impact of these words is blunted by their confusing association with phrases later in this fourth chapter such as "devote yourselves to prayer, being watchful and thankful" and "Tychicus will tell you all the news about me." The admonition to masters may remain the most memorable part of the chapter because of its leading position. Nevertheless, because it's been isolated from the rest of the section it belongs to, it will probably be misunderstood as a moralism or rule, rather than as one of three examples that illustrate a principle: in Christ, authority relationships involve reciprocal responsibilities.

What's true of Colossians is true of most other biblical books as well: the chapter divisions simply don't follow the inherent development of thought. If we did a similar analysis of 1 Corinthians, for example, we'd discover that long discussions of single topics have been broken up into chapters 1, 2, 3, and 4; into chapters 8, 9, and 10; and into chapters 12, 13, and 14. On the other hand, chapter 6 contains two separate discussions, as do chapters 7 and 11, while chapter 16 contains another short discussion plus an explanation of Paul's travel plans and some greetings. Only chapters 5 and 15 consist entirely of a single discussion. So the chapter divisions shouldn't be accepted uncritically as a reliable guide to the outline of 1 Corinthians. This example illustrates that it would unwise to do this for any other book, either.

Modern publishers, as I noted in the introduction, try to overcome the effects of badly placed chapter divisions by extending paragraphs right through them. However, our habits of reading tend to counteract the help that publishers are providing. We typically approach books of the Bible chapter-by-chapter anyway, whether in daily devotions, or in a weekly Bible study, or as a Scripture lesson for a sermon. And during more informal reading, those large, bold chapter numbers still act as "stop signs," even in the middle of a paragraph.

Chapter divisions were basically introduced to the Bible to help readers locate passages, and so they're designed to be generally all the same length. As a result, as we've just seen, they often break up longer sections, or else combine two or more shorter ones. Reading just a chapter at a time often forces us to treat only part of a longer section as if it were complete in itself, or else to treat two separate sections as if they made sense together as a single unit. This can't be done on the author's own terms, because the author never intended these sections to be divided or combined in this way.

Chapters do make sense in some books, such as Psalms, where they basically do correspond to inherent divisions, in this case, between songs that were written on different occasions by various authors. Even in Psalms, however, the chapter divisions aren't perfect. It's quite likely that Psalms 9 and 10 were originally a single psalm that has now been split in two, and that Psalms 42 and 43 were also originally just one psalm. In most other biblical books, chapters seriously obscure the original units of thought, rather than help us recognize them.

And even when chapter divisions do manage to hit the "seams" in a biblical book pretty well (as is sometimes the case), they still hinder our reading in a further way. They mask the existence of units that are larger than even potentially well-divided chapters. In other words, there may be a higher level of literary organization in a biblical book, above the "chapter" level. On this level we would find larger units made up of several chapters. But because chapters always appear to be the largest units in a book, even when they're good, they're usually still bad, because they keep us from recognizing these larger units.

For example, when we consider the laws in Leviticus, we discover that they've been grouped together by subject matter, such as leprosy, or clean and unclean foods, or festivals. We also find that these groups of laws are typically marked at their beginning or end with summary phrases that identify their content: "These are the regulations for the guilt offering" or "So Moses announced to the Israelites the appointed festivals of the LORD." For the most part, the chapters of Leviticus correspond well to this subject matter: they contain one group of laws on a given subject. A few dietary laws have not been shaved off the end of their group, for example, and included instead with the childbirth laws. These groups-of-laws are therefore among the "best" chapters in the Bible, in that they generally respect the inherent divisions in Leviticus.

Nevertheless, these chapters still keep us from following the book's overall outline, which actually consists of groups of groups-of-laws, organized according to a series of larger themes. For example, certain foods (chapter 11), childbirth (chapter 12), skin diseases (chapters 13–14), and bodily discharges (chapter 15) can all cause "uncleanness." These four groups-of-laws have therefore been put together in a larger section of the book that has to do with uncleanness. This "group of groups-of-laws" represents a literary division above the chapter (or "group-of-laws") level. As I've argued in an article,[6] the book can be understood to have four of these large divisions. But the twenty-seven chapters represent its highest divisions in most readers' eyes, and so they have no opportunity to appreciate this structure or to understand the book's contents in light of it.

The chapters in Matthew similarly keep us from recognizing a higher level of literary structure. As I've argued in another article,[7] the material in Matthew is basically organized, at its highest level, by genre. Story and speech alternate. The main narrative is repeatedly punctuated by long discourses. Five of these discourses are specially marked by an opening formula, which describes the disciples coming to Jesus for instruction, and also by a closing formula, "When Jesus had finished saying these things." In my analysis, each of these discourses takes up a theme that's introduced by the action in the preceding part of the narrative. This gospel thus considers in turn the foundations, mission, mystery, family, and destiny of the "kingdom of heaven." It begins with a genealogy (the list of Jesus' ancestors) and ends with the story of Jesus' arrest, trial, crucifixion, and resurrection (these events make up the "passion narrative").

According to this interpretation, at its highest level, Matthew consists of five narrative-discourse pairs, surrounded by introductory and concluding material:

Genealogy

Foundations Narrative - Foundations Discourse

Mission Narrative - Mission Discourse

Mystery Narrative - Mystery Discourse

Family Narrative - Family Discourse

Destiny Narrative - Destiny Discourse

Passion Narrative

There's no way to recognize this structure, however, or to understand Matthew's contents in light of it, by approaching it as a book with twenty-eight "chapters." This is true even though these chapters, once again, are pretty good. They typically respect the "seams" in this larger outline. The start of a discourse always begins a new chapter, for example, even if some discourses are divided into more than one chapter. The problem is that larger units in the book are being broken up and hidden by these chapters themselves.

There's another level of literary structure that chapters also obscure: the one below the chapter level. Chapters, at their best, correspond to the main sections of a shorter book, or to subsections of a longer book. But below these sections or subsections there usually are smaller units. In Leviticus, for example, as we've just seen, the chapters represent subsections of larger sections that deal with major themes such as cleanness. But these chapters are made up of many smaller parts—individual laws. For example, this law represents a unit of literary structure within Leviticus below the chapter level:

> When anyone brings a grain offering to the LORD, your offering is to be of the finest flour. You are to pour olive oil on it, put incense on it and take it to Aaron's sons the priests. The priest shall take a handful of the flour and oil, together with all the incense, and burn this as a memorial portion on the altar, a food offering, an aroma pleasing to the LORD. The rest of the grain offering belongs to Aaron and his sons; it is a most holy part of the food offering presented to the LORD.

Chapters and verses keep us from recognizing units on this level as well, since chapters divide a book into larger sections, while verses divide it into smaller ones. (The law just quoted is divided into three verses, Lev. 2:1–3.) However, it isn't so difficult for readers to recognize the units on this level, since many Bible publishers now divide the text into sections that are larger than verses but smaller than chapters. Nevertheless, we as readers should still come to our own conclusions about whether these divisions really do correspond to the actually intended units below the chapter level. And we should be aware that sections marked off by modern publishers can create some of the very same problems that chapters do, such as obscuring the existence of larger literary units, and encouraging us to approach the Bible as if it were a compendium of short devotional selections, rather than a library of whole literary works.

Since many Bibles already do give some indication of the literary units below the chapter level, our greater challenge, as readers and students of the Scriptures, is to recognize and appreciate the higher levels of organization in biblical books. This challenge has been discussed in some books on effective Bible reading. Grant Osborne, for example, stresses the importance of "charting a book" to identify its higher and lower levels of organization, above and below the chapters. He explains that we should try to trace the "thought development" of a whole book, and produce an outline that identifies its "major units." He warns:

> We must remember that verse and chapter divisions were never inspired. . . . The problem is that [scribes] often chose both verse and chapter divisions poorly, yet people tend to assume that [their] decisions were correct and interpret verses and chapters apart from the context around them.[8]

(The problem may also be that people don't realize these divisions aren't the work of the original authors.)

In the same way, Kay Arthur teaches readers to identify the level of organization above chapters, that is, to describe the "segments" or "major divisions" in a book of the Bible. She warns, "You don't subjectively create segment divisions. Rather, you discover them from the text."[9] She also trains readers to look for units that are smaller than chapters. She warns that these may not correspond to the publisher's paragraph divisions, and that they may run across the chapter divisions, which are "man made," and can be misleading.[10]

Unfortunately, such disciplined habits are not typical of the way most of us read or study the Scriptures. Instead, it's much more common for us to approach the Bible through its traditional chapter divisions. Home study groups often take up a chapter a week; ministers doing expository series typically preach through a book chapter by chapter; personal Bible reading schedules often prescribe a certain number of chapters a day. In fact, while we probably often feel a little uncomfortable or even guilty with the way we quote verses (asking ourselves, "Might this be a 'text out of context that's really a pretext'?"), we tend to consider chapter-based approaches much more rigorous and trustworthy. We need to be aware, therefore, of all the ways that chapter divisions can keep us from appreciating form, and thus meaning, as we read the Bible.

Verse divisions create even further problems for our understanding of the Bible. For one thing, just as chapters typically fail to correspond with the intermediate-sized units in biblical books, even though they're often about the same size, so verses, which are typically of sentence length, tend not to respect the sentence-sized divisions of thought within the biblical writings. Anyone who's been reading the Bible for even a short time has no doubt noticed many individual examples of how verse divisions can break up sentences and phrases that belong together, or else combine ones that should be kept separate.

For example, the statements numbered 1 Corinthians 6:19–20 in the traditional system, if divided reasonably into two verses, would read something like this:

> (19) Do you not know that your bodies are temples of the Holy Spirit, who is in you, whom you have received from God?
> (20) You are not your own; you were bought at a price. Therefore honor God with your bodies.

Unfortunately, the verse divisions were placed here instead:

> (19) Do you not know that your bodies are temples of the Holy Spirit, who is in you, whom you have received from God? You are not your own;
> (20) you were bought at a price. Therefore honor God with your bodies.

In Psalm 42–43, to give another example, a refrain is repeated three times:

> Why, my soul, are you downcast?
> Why so disturbed within me?
>
> Put your hope in God,
> for I will yet praise him,
> my Savior and my God.

The second and third time this refrain appears, it's a single verse. But the first time it appears, the words "and my God" are sliced off from the end of the last line and assigned to the following verse.

Verses also combine sentences and phrases that should be kept separate. At one point in 1 Corinthians, the apostle Paul wants to show that as believers, we're free not to insist on our rights, if we think giving them up will help further the gospel. Paul first establishes that he and his fellow apostles have the right to be paid for their work. Then, in a major transition, he reminds the Corinthians, "But we did not use this right." However, because there's no verse break, readers can miss the fact that a major transition occurs at this point. First Corinthians 9:12 combines this transitional statement with the end of the preceding part of Paul's argument:

> If others have this right of support from you, shouldn't we have it all the more? But we did not use this right. On the contrary, we put up with anything rather than hinder the gospel of Christ.

(Contemporary publishers often put a paragraph break in the middle of this verse, to help readers recognize the transition.)

These are only a few of the many examples that could be given to show how verse divisions inappropriately divide or combine sentences and phrases. But verse divisions can also distort our understanding of how sentences and phrases work together to create overall meaning within a longer passage. For example, the Ten Commandments, cited here from Exodus, would be divided most logically this way, with one commandment per verse:

> And God spoke all these words: I am the LORD your God, who brought you out of Egypt, out of the land of slavery.
>
> 1 You shall have no other gods before me.
>
> 2 You shall not make for yourself an image in the form of anything in heaven above or on the earth beneath or in the waters below. You shall not bow down to them or worship them; for I, the LORD your God, am a jealous God, punishing the children for the sin of the parents to the third and fourth generation of those who hate me, but showing love to a thousand generations of those who love me and keep my commandments.
>
> 3 You shall not misuse the name of the LORD your God, for the LORD will not hold anyone guiltless who misuses his name.
>
> 4 Remember the Sabbath day by keeping it holy. Six days you shall labor and do all your work, but the seventh day is a sabbath to the LORD your God. On it you shall not do any work, neither you, nor your son or daughter, nor your male or female servant, nor your animals, nor any foreigner residing in your towns. For in six days the LORD made the heavens and the earth, the sea, and all that is in them, but he rested on the seventh day. Therefore the LORD blessed the Sabbath day and made it holy.

5   Honor your father and your mother, so that
    you may live long in the land the LORD your
    God is giving you.

6   You shall not murder.

7   You shall not commit adultery.

8   You shall not steal.

9   You shall not give false testimony against your
    neighbor.

10 You shall not covet your neighbor's house.
    You shall not covet your neighbor's wife, or
    his male or female servant, his ox or donkey,
    or anything that belongs to your neighbor.

However, the traditional verses divide the Ten
Commandments this way instead, presenting them as
Exodus 20:1–17:

1   And God spoke all these words.

2   I am the LORD your God, who brought you out
    of Egypt, out of the land of slavery.

3   You shall have no other gods before me.

4   You shall not make for yourself an image in
    the form of anything in heaven above or on
    the earth beneath or in the waters below.

5   You shall not bow down to them or worship
    them; for I, the LORD your God, am a jealous
    God, punishing the children for the sin of the
    parents to the third and fourth generation of
    those who hate me,

6   but showing love to a thousand gen-
    erations of those who love me and keep my
    commandments.

7   You shall not misuse the name of the LORD
    your God, for the LORD will not hold anyone
    guiltless who misuses his name.

8   Remember the Sabbath day by keeping it holy.

9   Six days you shall labor and do all your work,

10 but the seventh day is a sabbath to the LORD
    your God. On it you shall not do any work,
    neither you, nor your son or daughter, nor
    your male or female servant, nor your animals,
    nor any foreigner residing in your towns.

11 For in six days the LORD made the heavens
    and the earth, the sea, and all that is in them,
    but he rested on the seventh day. Therefore
    the LORD blessed the Sabbath day and made it
    holy.

12 Honor your father and your mother, so that
    you may live long in the land the LORD your
    God is giving you.

13 You shall not murder.

14 You shall not commit adultery.

15 You shall not steal.

16 You shall not give false testimony against your
    neighbor.

17 You shall not covet your neighbor's house.
    You shall not covet your neighbor's wife, or
    his male or female servant, his ox or donkey,
    or anything that belongs to your neighbor.

At least some of the force of the Ten Commandments
derives from the fact that ten is the number of humanity in the Bible and in popular understanding (because

people typically have ten fingers and ten toes). Indeed, the Ten Commandments aren't so much a list of rules as a call for humans, as humans, to acknowledge the worship and obedience they owe to God as their Creator and Redeemer. (They recall that "the LORD made the heavens and the earth" and they speak of "your God, who brought you out of Egypt.") In other words, the *form* of the Ten Commandments helps us understand their *purpose*. But this form is obscured when they're divided into seventeen parts.

Further kinds of problems arise when we treat verses as independent, free-standing statements. For one thing, they permit and even encourage us to treat the Bible as a collection of isolated fragments that we can gather and arrange to support various viewpoints.

When I was a pastor, one of my parishioners invited me over to see the new Bible program he'd just gotten for his computer. He proudly demonstrated its features as I looked on. One feature was a search-by-topic function. The computer gave us a list of subjects in the Bible. By clicking on a word, we could get a series of verses to appear on the screen that dealt with that topic. The topics were in alphabetical order, and the first word was "alcohol." That seemed as good a place as any to begin, so I asked my friend to click on that word. The computer soon printed out a list of Bible verses that included:

- "Do not get drunk on wine, which leads to debauchery. Instead, be filled with the Spirit."

- "Wine is a mocker and beer a brawler; whoever is led astray by them is not wise."

- "Who has woe? Who has sorrow? Who has strife? Who has complaints? Who has needless bruises? Who has bloodshot eyes? Those who linger over wine, who go to sample bowls of mixed wine."

I looked over the list for a while and finally said, "You know, they left out a few."

My friend asked, "What do you mean?"

I replied, "Just look at the list."

Pretty soon a grin broke over his face. He said, "Oh yes," and recited, "Stop drinking only water, and use a little wine because of your stomach," from Paul's first letter to Timothy. My friend recognized that while the computer had been programmed to list only verses that warned against the abuse of alcohol (certainly a very important warning to provide), the Bible also says in several places that alcohol can have a positive use. I mentioned another place, the statement in Psalm 104 that God gives "wine that gladdens human hearts, oil to make their faces shine, and bread that sustains their hearts."

But there were other verses we could have cited, of an even different character. When we search its pages, we discover that the Bible actually contains some statements about alcohol that sound very troubling. For example, God commands the Israelites in Deuteronomy, "[E]xchange your tithe for silver, and take the silver with you and go to the place the LORD your God will choose. Use the silver to buy whatever you like: cattle, sheep, wine or other fermented drink, or anything you wish." Are we really to spend our tithe on liquor? There's an even more disturbing statement in King Lemuel's words in Proverbs: "Let beer be for those who are perishing, wine for those who are in anguish! Let them drink and forget their poverty and remember their misery no more." Does God really want people to escape from their problems through drunkenness? And does God want us to encourage this behavior on the part of the poor, rather than helping them escape from poverty?

Not really. When we read these verses from Proverbs in light of their broader context, we discover that there's genuine concern for the poor in this passage. The Bible isn't condoning drunkenness. The full passage reads:

> It is not for kings, Lemuel—
> it is not for kings to drink wine,
> nor for rulers to crave beer,

> lest they drink and forget what has been decreed,
> and deprive all the oppressed of their rights.

> Let beer be for those who are perishing,
> wine for those who are in anguish!

> Let them drink and forget their poverty
> and remember their misery no more.

> Speak up for those who cannot speak for
>   themselves,
> for the rights of all who are destitute.

> Speak up and judge fairly;
> defend the rights of the poor and needy.

The real teaching here, in other words, is that kings

41

shouldn't get drunk, because if they do, they'll pervert justice, and the poor and needy will not be helped. The two verses that sounded so troubling by themselves are actually a rhetorical flourish within this longer passage. They're saying, in effect, "Hey, if anybody's got to get drunk, let it be those with something to forget, not those who have to stay sharp for everyone's sake." But we shouldn't infer from this that anybody's really got to get drunk.

In the same way, by studying the tithe regulations in Deuteronomy, we could show that it wouldn't really be proper for Christians today to spend their tithe on liquor for a party. Just as importantly, if we studied all the verses the computer did select, we'd see that they don't really present a biblical imperative for total abstinence from alcohol, as the search results seemed to imply. Rather, they warn against the *abuse* of alcohol: "don't *get drunk* . . . don't *tarry long* over wine . . . don't be *led astray* by it." Total abstinence is still a personal conviction that many Christians will adopt as a way of honoring God. Nevertheless, the Bible's counsel concerning drinking is essentially that in this area of life, as in all areas, we should cultivate self-control, whether this means abstinence or sober moderation.

How, then, might this computer program have left the impression that the Bible's counsel is total abstinence? It did so by selecting and arranging certain verses. If this was done deliberately, this was no doubt with the best of intentions. There's a long-standing and well-respected tradition of abstinence teaching in the church. The Bible itself tells us that one may abstain as a matter of personal conviction and sensitivity to the weaknesses of others. "It is better not to eat meat or drink wine or to do anything else that will cause your brother or sister to fall," Paul told the Romans. Nevertheless, we must insist that verses should not be selected and arranged to create the impression that a matter of personal conviction or traditional emphasis is the Bible's counsel to everyone.

Indeed, verses shouldn't be selected and arranged to create the impression that the Bible teaches anything it really doesn't. But because verses divide the Bible up into little "sound bites," which can be located and quoted without regard to their context, they practically invite us to select and arrange isolated statements in support of our favorite teachings, whether or not their context actually supports the meaning we're imputing to them.

Treating verses as free-standing units encourages other unreliable approaches to the Bible as well. When we encounter verses as isolated phrases, we tend to understand them the way we would if they'd been written today, rather than the way they were originally intended.

For example, in one adult Sunday School class I taught, we were discussing Jesus' statement in the Sermon on the Mount that God "sends rain on the righteous and the unrighteous." The members of the class took "rain" as a reference to the problems of life, since that's what it usually means to us (as, for example, in the popular saying, "Into every life a little rain must fall"). And so the class began to talk about why bad things happen to good people. But as we looked at Matthew more closely, we realized that the "rain" Jesus was talking about was actually a good thing:

together with the sun, it brought about a good harvest. Our real question should have been, "Why do good things happen to bad people?" (The short answer is, "Because God is kind.")

We probably give the verses we quote a contemporary meaning, rather than their original meaning, far more often than we realize. One year at Christmas time a friend of mine went into a Christian bookstore and saw a large banner that read, "Celebrate by sending each other gifts, Revelation 11:10." That sounded like a wonderful thought for the season until she looked this statement up in her Bible. She discovered it was actually a description of how the enemies of God will rejoice over the death of the "two witnesses": they will "refuse them burial," and "the inhabitants of the earth will gloat over them and *celebrate by sending each other gifts*." Many other examples like this could be given, but the point should be clear: verses not only encourage selection and arrangement, they also encourage reading apart from context so that the reader, not the text, supplies the meaning in the end.

In fact, even when we understand the meaning of the words in an isolated statement the way they would have been understood in their original *historical* context, we may still misunderstand the statement because we fail to appreciate it within its *literary* context (that is, within the author's developing argument). We saw an example of this earlier: the statement "let beer be for those who are perishing . . . let them drink and forget their poverty" is not a positive command for us to ply the poor with liquor. It's simply a contrast to the point that "it is not for kings to drink wine, nor for rulers to crave beer." In other words, verses break up the thoughts of the biblical authors. This causes us to understand these thoughts only partially, and often to misunderstand them.

There's yet another problem with treating verses as intentional units. Verses can be pitted against one another in discussions or disputes, and this can create the impression that the Bible contradicts itself. This prevents the Bible from being a reliable source of guidance, either because we don't know which verse to follow, or because we lose confidence in the Bible entirely.

I was visiting a friend's church one Sunday when the special feature was a puppet show. In the show, a boy named Billy was worried because his father had lost his job. At one of Billy's shoulders stood a devil puppet, who was trying to convince him that God didn't want his father to get another job. The devil puppet asked, "Doesn't the Bible say, 'Blessed are you who are poor'?" At the other shoulder was an angel puppet, who countered that Billy should take his concerns to God in prayer. This angel quoted from Philippians: "Do not be anxious about anything, but in every situation, by prayer and petition, with thanksgiving, present your requests to God. And the peace of God, which transcends all understanding, will guard your hearts and your minds in Christ Jesus." As soon as Billy heard the angel say this, he prayed and experienced the peace of Christ. All of us in the audience nodded in approval. (And eventually, his father did get a job.)

This was a wonderful lesson for the children that the puppet show was intended for, and for the rest of us as well: we should trust God and pray in troubling times. But on what basis did Billy, and we, know that prayer was the right thing for him to do in his family's situation? The devil and the angel were actually using the same approach to the Bible: quoting verses. So how was Billy to know which verse to follow? Should he accept the situation and be grateful for the spiritual blessings his family was about to receive through poverty ("blessed are you who are poor")? Or should he try to change the situation, "presenting his requests" to God through intercessory prayer? Our own experience may have led us to the conclusion that prayer was the right approach: we may have been unemployed ourselves at some point, and so didn't think it was something God would have wanted for Billy's father, at least not for the long term. Or we might have remembered the many times we in our churches had prayed for people who needed jobs. We might even have known that the devil puppet was actually quoting Jesus out of context. Jesus didn't say that the poor are blessed because they were in want, he said they were blessed because they weren't in a place of earthly privilege that made them resistant to the gospel. But we couldn't have reached the right conclusion by relating to the Bible on the verse level, because on that level, it's ambiguous. The two verses quoted in the puppet show, if considered as isolated statements, point in opposite directions for someone in Billy's situation. And if we never leave the verse level, this ambiguity can only be resolved by something other than the Bible. When this happens, the

Bible ceases to be our primary authority; something else inevitably takes its place.

In other words, when we take "Bible verses" as statements that can meaningfully stand alone, apart from their context, this allows and even encourages us to develop bad habits of reading and study. These bad habits can ultimately lead us to substitute our own teachings and understandings for those of the Bible. This happens in several ways: through selection and arrangement; through reading in isolation; and in response to the impression that the Bible's counsel is contradictory.

Furthermore, even if we don't substitute our own teachings for the Bible's, verses may encourage us to understand even biblical teachings in unbiblical ways. Verses encourage us to read one statement at a time, and so they encourage legal and intellectual readings of the Bible, as if it essentially contained rules for us to follow, or doctrines for us to believe. But obeying the Bible's teachings doesn't mean following a set of rules or embracing a set of beliefs. Rather, because the Bible is essentially seeking to introduce us to God, obeying the Bible's teaching means, before anything else, entering into a personal relationship with God, and then having our minds and characters transformed as that relationship grows and deepens.

We've seen how the division of the biblical text into short snippets encourages bad habits of reading that lead to irresponsible use of the Scriptures. All of this would be bad enough even if verses managed to respect the sentence-level divisions of thought within the biblical writings. But as we have seen, they typically don't.

Given all these problems with verses, we should be very concerned that we relate so frequently to the Bible on the verse level. We rely on topical lists of verses that we find in computer programs like my friend's and in "pocket promise books" and in the front or back sections of our Bibles. When we memorize the Bible, we usually do this a verse at a time. In our homes we have wall plaques, posters, calendars, and even coffee mugs that present Bible verses to us daily. The sermons we hear in church may send us flipping back and forth through the pages of our Bibles to find verses being cited in support of specific points. As we do, we may be using a translation that prints each verse as a separate paragraph. Even scholarly commentaries, written by interpreters who are well aware that the original authors didn't divide their works into chapters and verses, tend to go chapter-by-chapter and verse-by-verse through biblical books anyway, if only so their readers can turn conveniently to their comments on a particular passage. Indeed, it may be more common for believers to approach the Bible on the verse level than in any other way.

But so long as we continue this approach, we're permitting and encouraging people to substitute human traditions for the Bible's own counsel. We're not hearing genuinely from God, and we're not having a life-changing encounter with God through his word. No wonder our experience of Scripture isn't satisfying and enjoyable. No wonder it doesn't keep us coming back for more. And no wonder our younger generations, who think of truth as nonpropositional, narrative, and experiential (much closer to the way the Scriptures actually present the truth), are walking away from the Bible. We need to approach God's word in a new way.

If we want to understand the Bible on its own terms, we should relate to it properly not on the verse level, nor on the chapter level, but on the level of its individual books—particularly if we can set aside the signals we get from chapters and verses and appreciate all the levels of literary structure the biblical books actually have. The Bible is, after all, essentially a collection of literary creations. Their "book form" is thus their original form. However, the form the Bible has been given over time also creates problems even if we approach it on the book level. We'll explore this in our next chapter.

Chapter Two
The Problem with "Books"

L uke and Acts provide one of the clearest illustrations of the problems that the historical reshaping
of the Bible creates on the book level. When these
two volumes are read together, it's clear that they're parts
of a single work. They're united by an overarching literary structure. As L.T. Johnson observes, their author

> uses geography to structure his story and to
> advance his literary and theological goals.
> . . . In the Gospel, the narrative moves *toward*
> Jerusalem. . . . In Acts, the geographic movement
> is *away from* Jerusalem. . . . The middle twelve
> chapters of the two-volume work narrate events
> exclusively in that place.[1]

In other words, Luke and Acts are held together by this
structure:

> *Journey to Jerusalem*
>
> *Events in Jerusalem*
>
> *Journey from Jerusalem*

Luke–Acts is a two-volume historical study that's designed to let believers "know the certainty of the things you have been taught" about the life of Jesus and the work of his followers. Some distinction between Luke and Acts is appropriate. The writer himself, in the dedication to Theophilus at the start of the second volume, refers back to the first volume as his *protos logos*, the "first section"[2] of his historical narrative. But the two parts should still be read together, as a single literary composition. Unfortunately, because they're no longer attached to one another in our Bibles, they're almost always read and studied separately. In fact, they're typically regarded as "different books," as if they'd been written for different purposes on different occasions. But when we approach them that way, we lose sight of the structural and thematic unity they have as the two halves of a single work. Recognizing this unity would inform and enrich our reading of each volume.

The idea that Luke and Acts are two different books is reinforced by the traditional order of the books of the Bible. John, an entirely separate composition by another author, has been placed between them. This arrangement encourages us to think of Luke as a book that belongs with Matthew, Mark, and John, but not with Acts. In our minds we put Luke in a group of "gospels," and think of Acts as belonging by itself as "history." In other words, readers who might otherwise recognize Luke–Acts as a whole literary creation are misdirected, both by the division of this two-volume work into distinct parts, and by the way one volume is assigned to a collection of writings from which the other is excluded.

Beyond even this, different kinds of titles have been given to the two volumes, and these titles create the impression that Luke and Acts are actually different kinds of writing. The first volume's full traditional title is "The Gospel of Luke" or "The Gospel According to Luke." This implies that it's the kind of writing (genre) known as "gospel." The second volume has been entitled "The Acts of the Apostles," suggesting that it is a work that relates the "acts" of one or more notable people. This is a well-attested genre in Greco-Roman literature. David Aune, in *The New Testament in Its Literary Environment*, notes examples such as Callisthenes' *Acts of Alexander* and Sosylus's *Acts of Hannibal*. Aune concludes, however, that "[t]he term offers little help in determining the genre of the book of Acts." Instead, he suggests, Luke's most influential model for this work was provided by the "general history," which "focused on the history of a particular people . . . from mythical beginnings to a point in the recent past."[3] Luke is actually writing a two-volume general history of the "kingdom of God" that has begun to arrive on earth. And so we shouldn't consider Acts a book that relates first the "acts" of Peter, then the "acts" of Philip, and finally the "acts" of Paul, even though its traditional title encourages us to do this. Instead, we need to recognize this volume as the continuation of a "general history" that begins in Luke.

In all these ways, the reshaping of the Bible encourages us to read these two volumes as if they were separate books and different kinds of writing. This kind of distortion puts a huge obstacle in the way of people who'd be able to hear the Bible's message much more clearly if they could recognize and engage the whole literary creations that have been collected in the Scriptures.

We concluded in Chapter 1 that we should approach the Bible on the book level, not on the chapter or verse level. But as we've already begun to see here, the historical reshaping of the Bible can actively obscure form and meaning even on the book level. As illustrated by the case of Luke–Acts, this can happen through:

- the way some longer books have been divided into two or more parts;

- the order the books of the Bible have been put in; and

- the titles the biblical books have been given.

These factors often promote interpretations that the text of a book, if encountered without them, wouldn't support. Specifically, they can lead us to assume the wrong things about who wrote a book and why, who a book was written to, and what it's about. These factors can also keep us from recognizing what kind of writing a book is, and how it's put together. We'll now consider the history and effects of the book divisions, order, and titles in the Bible in greater detail. This will help us become more aware of their effects and of what needs to be done to overcome them.

Book *divisions*—indications of where one book ends and another begins—are one important aspect of the Bible's historical reshaping that can obscure its form and meaning. We shouldn't always assume that we've finished a literary composition when we've reached the end of a biblical "book." In some cases, the book divisions we know, like chapter and verse divisions, don't correspond with the works the biblical authors composed, because longer works have been broken up into several parts. In other words, the "problem with books" in the Bible as we know it today begins with the fact that many of the "books" aren't really books at all.

We saw in Chapter 1 how chapter divisions can keep us from recognizing large units that stretch across several chapters within a biblical book. In the same way, some of the traditional book divisions in the Bible can keep us from recognizing even larger units that now stretch across two or more "books." These traditional divisions were introduced when several originally unified compositions in the Old Testament were separated into parts so they could be accommodated conveniently on the scrolls of their day. These parts have now come to be treated as complete books in themselves. But they really shouldn't be understood this way. Instead, we should put these parts back together and re-create the original literary wholes, so we can understand and appreciate them as we were intended to.

For example, the four "books" we now know as 1 and 2 Samuel and 1 and 2 Kings are actually the parts that an originally unified composition, Samuel–Kings, has been divided into. Because of its length, this work was first separated into two parts, "Samuel" and "Kings," in the original Hebrew. (These are still just two books in Hebrew Bibles today.) When the Old Testament was translated into Greek, it became one-third longer, and it was difficult to fit even these parts on single scrolls of a convenient size. So they were both divided again, into 1 and 2 Samuel and 1 and 2 Kings.

The structuring pattern that tied the original work together still runs through all four of these parts. It's created by a series of notices about kings and their reigns. These notices tell us how old a king was when he came to the throne, how many years he ruled, and in what place. A typical example is: "David was thirty years old when he became king, and he reigned forty years. In Hebron he reigned over Judah seven years and six months, and in Jerusalem he reigned over all Israel and Judah thirty-three years."

These notices serve as introductions (or sometimes conclusions) to descriptions of each king's character and the notable events and achievements of his reign. These descriptions vary greatly in length. The reigns of Saul, David, and Solomon are considered in much more detail than those of the other kings. But these descriptions of kings and their reigns, marked at the beginning or end by a recurring formula, are the highest-level literary units, the basic building blocks, that were put together to create a single work, Samuel–Kings. We shouldn't let the way we now encounter this material in four separate "books," with two different kinds of names, keep us from recognizing that it was all originally a single composition.

Indeed, we should recognize that the current divisions between these "books" actually break up the basic building blocks of the original composition in every case. The division between 1 and 2 Samuel comes a little bit before the notice that introduces Ish-Bosheth's reign. This division thus cuts off part of Saul's reign and attaches it to the story of his son. Similarly, the break between 2 Samuel and 1 Kings comes a little before the notice that concludes David's reign.[4] This attaches the end of his reign to the beginning of Solomon's. And the notice that begins the account of Ahaziah's reign comes just before the start of 2 Kings, so that his reign is announced in one book and described in the next.

If these book divisions had been placed just a little bit earlier or later, they wouldn't have broken up the descriptions of reigns that are the basic building blocks of the entire work. Why, then, were they placed where they were? There seems to be one explanation in the case of the division of Samuel and Kings into two parts each, and a different explanation for the earlier division of the whole work into Samuel and Kings.

Second Samuel begins, "After the death of Saul," and 2 Kings begins, "After Ahab's death." This is reminiscent of the way Joshua begins, "After the death of Moses" and Judges begins, "After the death of Joshua." In other words, when Samuel and Kings were each divided in half after being translated into Greek, the people who placed the divisions may have been imitating what seemed like a suitable model in Joshua and Judges. But the references to the deaths of Saul and Ahab at the start of 2 Samuel and 2 Kings don't actually function *structurally* the way the references to the deaths of Moses and Joshua do at the start of Joshua and Judges. So we shouldn't look to these death notices in Samuel–Kings as literary-structural guides, even though they now represent "first lines" of "books."

As for the earlier division of the original work into "Samuel" and "Kings," a break seems to have been placed at a point where there's a pause, although not a full stop, in this long story of the Israelite monarchy. Before David's death is described, the work includes some material that looks back on the transition from Saul to David. This material is presented in a "chiasm," that is, a literary arrangement based on pairs of episodes nested within one another. Hebrew writers considered this arrangement beautiful and elegant. They used it at significant places in their works, like this one:

> **A** Guilt upon Israel because of Saul
>   **B** David's mighty men
>   **C** A song of David
>   **C** A song of David
>   **B** David's mighty men
> **A** Guilt upon Israel because of David

The parallel between the two "A" sections is reinforced by a repeated phrase. The first account ends, "After that, God answered prayer in behalf of the land," and the second account concludes, "Then the LORD answered [David's] prayer in behalf of the land."

This presentation of largely non-narrative material does create an artful pause in the story. But we should still recognize that placing a book break in this spot makes it more difficult to follow the structuring pattern that runs through all of Samuel–Kings. This pattern is supposed to help us understand and interpret all of the material it organizes into a unified composition.

Chronicles is another book that was divided in two when it was translated into Greek. In the Hebrew Bible, it's still just one book. And like Samuel or Kings, Chronicles itself is only part of an even longer work, whose other part has also been divided into two books: Ezra and Nehemiah. (Ezra–Nehemiah remained one book even in Greek translation; it was separated only later, when the Bible was translated into Latin.) We can tell that Chronicles and Ezra–Nehemiah were recognized in ancient times as parts of a single composition by the way they've been "stitched together." The first several dozen words of Ezra–Nehemiah have been copied onto the end of Chronicles.[5] This was how scribes indicated that a work that began on one scroll was continued on another.

When we read Chronicles–Ezra–Nehemiah as a single work, we recognize that it's essentially a "temple history." That is, even though it tells the story of the covenant people going all the way back to Adam, its main concern is with the temple that was built in Jerusalem, which God commanded the Jews to rebuild after the exile. (The temple and the worship in it are the specific focus of much of the material that's found in this work but absent from Samuel–Kings.) But this overall emphasis on the temple and its worship is difficult to appreciate now that the work has been divided into four parts that have three different titles, particularly since two of the titles suggest that their focus is on the careers of individuals (Ezra and Nehemiah).

There's also a single structuring pattern that begins early in Exodus, runs all the way through Leviticus, and extends nearly to the end of Numbers. It shouldn't surprise us that a pattern like this should tie all of this material together, since Exodus, Leviticus, and Numbers are three of the five parts that an originally longer work, the Torah, was divided into. These divisions are ancient; they were introduced many centuries before Christ. But they are not so ancient as the literary material itself. Once again, the purpose of these "book" divisions was simply to allow the entire work to be contained on scrolls of a more convenient size. (Within Judaism today, these books together are still called the "five-fifths of the Torah.")

This long central section of the Torah, which begins when the Israelites leave Egypt and continues until they reach the borders of the land of Canaan, is structured by travel notices. These notices report movement from one place to another, for example: "The Israelites journeyed from Rameses to Sukkoth"; "After leaving Sukkoth they camped at Etham on the edge of the desert." After each notice there's a description of what happened at that stop on the journey. These descriptions actually constitute the highest-level units in this section of the Torah. But these units are of greatly varying lengths. Some are as short as a single sentence: "Then they came to Elim, where there were twelve springs and seventy palm trees, and they camped there near the water." But one unit, sometimes called the Sinai Pericope (because it's the account of what happened while the Israelites were at Mount Sinai), actually constitutes the vast bulk of this section. This unit extends from the middle of Exodus well into Numbers. Thus, when seen within this structural framework based on travel notices, the "book" of Leviticus is only part of one unit (the Sinai Pericope) within one section of the Torah (the journey to Canaan).

A case can still be made for treating Leviticus as a coherent whole. It describes its own content very succinctly in a concluding summary: "These are the decrees, the laws and the regulations that the LORD established on Mount Sinai between himself and the Israelites through Moses." In other words, Leviticus is an ordered collection of the laws God gave Moses while the Israelites were at Mount Sinai. As such, it can be meaningfully studied as a whole. As I noted in Chapter 1, I've described in an article at least one way it can be seen to have an elegant structure of its own.[6] But to understand Leviticus within its full literary context, we should also recognize the wider framework it's been placed in. We shouldn't let the traditional book boundaries and book names keep us from appreciating this setting.

But even as we seek to approach the Torah as a unified composition in order to understand its parts within their broader literary context, there's also a sense in which we do need to see it as the "five books" of Moses. The Torah was divided into five parts so early in the course of the Bible's formation that later biblical authors and editors sometimes mirrored this shape in their own works, to show that they were Scripture too. The division of Psalms into five "books," for example, seems intended to encourage people to read and reflect on this group of songs the same way they would read the Torah. (This message is reinforced by the way Psalm 1, at the start of the collection, encourages meditation on the "law of the Lord.") Lamentations may similarly present five poems about the destruction of Jerusalem in order to echo the shape of the Torah. And Jesus may be depicted in Matthew as the "new Moses" by the way his teachings have been organized into five "books."

So the division of the Torah into five parts has been reflected in the Scriptures in various places, and this can help inform our understanding of other books in the Bible. But everything we've said about the value of approaching the Torah as a unified composition still holds. In fact, the historical shaping of the Bible testifies just as clearly to the unity of this work as to its division. We see this, for example, in the way these "books" are known in Hebrew by their opening words, instead of by individual titles. (I'll say more about this shortly.)

So as we read Samuel–Kings, Chronicles–Ezra–Nehemiah and the Torah, we need to be aware of the ways that traditional book divisions can keep us from recognizing that what seem like a number of different books are actually one unified composition. This, as I've said, is much like the way chapter divisions can keep us from recognizing larger literary units within biblical books.

But as we've seen, chapter divisions can also mislead us by combining smaller separate units, and book divisions can do the same thing. Specifically, the so-called "minor prophets" are sometimes treated as if they were a coherent literary unity, the "Book of the Twelve." In other words, the equivalent of a book boundary is often drawn around them. This can happen either formally, as when commentaries are written on this "Book of the Twelve," or informally, when we group "all of those minor prophets" together in our minds.

Placing a boundary around the minor prophets—treating these individual books as smaller units within a larger literary whole—actively undermines their message and meaning. As Herbert Marks has observed,

> The final count of twelve prophets seems less a reflection of the material available than a deliberately imposed convention, designed to enforce a radical kind of closure. . . . In the Hebrew arrangement . . . the Twelve come immediately after the three "major" prophets, Isaiah, Jeremiah and Ezekiel. The pattern of three plus twelve recalls the three patriarchs and the twelve sons of Jacob—one of the basic paradigms of Israelite historiography. . . . By accommodating the prophetic corpus to such a type, the editors were in effect assimilating prophecy to a canonical rule, solidly rooted in communal tradition. . . . From this perspective, "The Book of the Twelve" may well be an anti-prophetic document, restricting prophecy to a limited number of sources, whose authority depends on established precedent.[7]

In other words, this is a case where a book boundary creates a form that undermines the meaning of the writings it shapes: creating a "Book of the Twelve" shuts down prophecy rather than encouraging it. So the separate books of the "minor prophets" shouldn't be combined this way, either formally or informally.

This is particularly true since no overarching structural pattern ties the "minor prophets" together. Instead, the book boundary in this case was once again created because of scroll length: it was more convenient to copy several short books together onto a single scroll than to create a tiny scroll for each one.

But almost-mystical considerations also seem to have had an influence. In the second century, the scholar-theologian Origen wrote in his commentary on the Psalms that "the canonical books are twenty-two, according to the Hebrew tradition."[8] He then listed the books, showing how he arrived at this number. Origen listed single books of Samuel and Kings, and of Chronicles and Ezra–Nehemiah, reflecting the first stage in the division of the two longer works we've just discussed. In Origen's list Joshua and Judges are combined, as are Jeremiah and Lamentations. And he apparently also considered the minor prophets a single "Book of the Twelve,"[9] yielding a total of twenty-two Old Testament books. Why this number? Origen argued that it was "not without reason" that the books of the Hebrew Bible were

> the same in number as the letters of the Hebrew
> alphabet. For as the twenty-two letters may be
> regarded as an introduction to the wisdom and the
> Divine doctrines given to men in those Characters,
> so the twenty-two inspired books are an alphabet
> of the wisdom of God and an introduction to the
> knowledge of realities.[10]

In other words, there should be twenty-two books in the Hebrew Scriptures because there are twenty-two letters in the Hebrew alphabet.

Jerome, who lived some two centuries later, arrived at the same total in much the same way, and for the same reason. His list is identical to Origen's except that Ruth, rather than Joshua, is combined with Judges. In his *Prologue to the Book of Kings* Jerome observed that "just as there are twenty-two elements [letters], by which we write in Hebrew all that we say . . . thus twenty-two scrolls are counted, by which letters and writings a just man is instructed in the doctrine of God."[11] However, Jerome noted that others treated Ruth and Lamentations as distinct books, and thus reached a total of "twenty-four books of the Old Law." He observed that this was a figure that "the Apocalypse of John introduces with the number of twenty-four elders worshipping the Lamb and offering their crowns."[12] So Origen and Jerome established their book boundaries within the Bible, and particularly the one around the "Twelve Prophets," not by appreciating the structures that authors had built into books, but in order to reach totals with a mystical significance.

One other example of drawing book boundaries to reach a certain numerical total comes from the churches in Syria, Egypt, and Ethiopia that treat the final two collections of sayings in Proverbs as a separate book, the "Wisdom of Bagor" (that is, Agur).[13] It actually does make sense, on one level, not to include the sayings of Agur and Lemuel in a book that describes itself as "the proverbs of Solomon." However, even without these last two collections, Proverbs still includes sayings by authors other than Solomon. Two anonymous groups of "sayings of the wise" come between the two collections of Solomon's sayings. And the opening exhortations in the book may not have been written by him either, since they're followed by the introductory heading "the proverbs of Solomon" as the sayings themselves begin. The creation of a separate book from the sayings of Agur and Lemuel may therefore have been motivated not so much by a wish to include only sayings by Solomon in Proverbs as by an effort to create a "wisdom pentateuch." In the churches where the "Wisdom of Bagor" has been split off from Proverbs, the two resulting books are typically grouped together with Ecclesiastes, Ecclesiasticus, and Wisdom of Solomon. In other words, as in the case of Psalms (and perhaps Lamentations and Matthew), the authoritative character of writings is being proclaimed by a fivefold division that reflects the traditional shape of the Torah. Even as we acknowledge that the biblical wisdom books are authoritative (though Protestants would hold that Ecclesiasticus and Wisdom of Solomon aren't fully canonical), it must still be insisted that book boundaries shouldn't be determined by "Bible numerics" that invoke numbers like five, twenty-two, or twenty-four. Instead, book boundaries should be established by identifying distinct original compositions. This means that Samuel–Kings, Chronicles–Ezra–Nehemiah, Luke–Acts, and each of the minor prophets should be recognized as individual "books." It's also quite reasonable to leave the sayings of Agur and Lemuel in the book of Proverbs, since it's a multiple-author anthology anyway.

The *order* in which we're used to encountering the books of the Bible is another aspect of the Bible's historical reshaping that can impede our understanding of the Scriptures. For one thing, this order can obscure the *circumstances* under which books were composed—that is, who wrote them, and why.

Consider, for example, the effects of the order in which we're used to encountering Paul's letters. If we number Paul's epistles from the earliest to the latest, based on a plausible understanding of when they were written (scholarly estimates would vary in certain cases), we discover that the current arrangement presents them roughly in this sequence:

6, 3, 4, 5, 9, 10, 8, 1, 2, 11, 13, 12, 7.

This order actively discourages us from trying to understand Paul's letters as we should, within the context of his life and the development of his thought. Instead, it makes us encounter them more as rootless, ethereal documents. This is truly ironic, since so much in these letters is written to challenge and correct an otherworldly spirituality. The simple fact is that in the order we're used to, these epistles have been sorted into two groups, letters to churches and letters to individuals, and then arranged roughly by *length*, from longest to shortest, within each of these groups. This is no more helpful or meaningful an arrangement than the one a friend of mine discovered when he returned home from college after a family move. He went up to his new room to find that his mother had arranged his books by color! So we shouldn't grant this reshaping an authority that would allow its dehistoricizing effect on the Pauline corpus to continue unchecked. As G.C.D. Howley has noted,

> The arrangement of the letters of Paul in the New Testament is in general that of their length. When we rearrange them into their chronological order, fitting them as far as possible into their life-setting within the record of the Acts of the Apostles, they begin to yield up more of their treasure; they become self-explanatory, to a greater extent than when this background is ignored.[14]

The customary arrangement of the minor prophets similarly frustrates an attempt to understand these books within the context of the prophetic tradition as it developed over the centuries. For example, for greatest understanding, we should read Amos, Hosea, Micah, and at least the beginning of Isaiah together, since they all speak to the same historical situation in the eighth century BC. (J.B. Phillips encouraged just such a reading when he published his translations of these works in a single volume entitled *Four Prophets: Amos, Hosea, First Isaiah, Micah: A Modern Translation from the Hebrew.*[15]) But in the familiar order, Hosea is separated from Amos by the book of Joel, which could come from a much later time. And Amos is separated from Micah by the book of Obadiah, which was written nearly 150 years later, and by the book of Jonah, which could also date from a much later period (even though it relates eighth-century events). On top of all this, the oracles of these three eighth-century "minor" prophets (Amos, Hosea, and Micah) have been placed a great distance away from the oracles of Isaiah, who was their contemporary.

On what basis have the minor prophets been put in their traditional sequence? At least the first several books appear to have been ordered by catch phrases. Something at the end of one book sounds similar to something near the start of another book, so they're put together. Hosea, Joel, Amos, and Obadiah seem to have been put in that sequence based on this principle:

- "Return, Israel, to the LORD your God" near the end of Hosea connects with "'Even now,' declares the LORD, 'return to me with all your heart'" near the start of Joel.

- "The LORD will roar from Zion and thunder from Jerusalem" near the end of Joel connects with "The LORD roars from Zion and thunders from Jerusalem" at the start of Amos.

- "So that they may possess the remnant of Edom and all the nations that bear my name" near the end of Amos connects with "People from the Negev will occupy the mountains of Esau, and people from the foothills will possess the land of the Philistines" in Obadiah.

This principle of organization takes readers back and forth significantly through time as they move from one book to the next. This discourages an appreciation of these prophetic oracles within their historical contexts.

The placement of books within the customary order can also create unjustified expectations about their *genre*. James has been placed at the head of the "general epistles," which are, to all appearances, a group of letters composed by leading figures of the church (James, Peter, John, and Jude) and sent to wider audiences than Paul's epistles. The book of James does begin like a letter, since it's intended to be read and heard by believers scattered throughout the Roman Empire. But after its opening, it doesn't follow the standard epistolary format, which would have included a thanksgiving and prayer, followed by the main body of the letter, and then closing elements such as greetings. James instead offers just a mixture of short sayings and slightly longer discussions of practical subjects. While there is thematic continuity, there's no sequential development. In these ways the book of James actually has strong affinities with the wisdom literature of the Old Testament. We should therefore approach it the same way we'd approach a book like Proverbs. But the placement of James within the "general epistles" encourages us to try to read it like a letter instead.

We need to be equally careful about our expectations of genre as we read the book of Jonah. Jonah was a prophet, and the book of Jonah is a book about a prophet. But it's not a book of prophecy. That is, it's not a collection of poetic oracles, like most of the rest of the prophetic books. It's a biographical narrative. True, there are biographical narratives in some of the other prophetic books, but the story of Jonah is different. In it, the prophet plays a symbolic role, emblematic of the nation of Israel. For the purposes of this book, that role is actually more significant than Jonah's identity as a historical figure who brought the "word of the LORD" to the people at a specific point in time. In a few other cases, prophets played roles in which they symbolized the nation; Ezekiel, for example, was commanded to live on siege rations for over a year to announce the impending siege of Jerusalem. But when other prophets performed signs or served as signs in this way, this was in obedience to God's commands. Jonah actually serves as a sign because of his disobedience. (God didn't say to him, "Behold, I am sending you to Nineveh, but you shall flee to Tarshish instead, and when the people ask you, 'Why have you fled to Tarshish,' you shall say to them, 'Thus are you doing, O Israel . . .'") The reader must make judgments throughout the story about what Jonah is doing, and why, and whether it's appropriate; in the end, the reader is actually meant to adopt an attitude opposite to Jonah's. In that sense, in its literary form at least, Jonah is actually is more like the books in the wisdom tradition than the ones in the prophetic tradition, since it works by analogy, just as the parables and proverbs of wisdom writing do.

Jonah therefore represents something of a special case among the prophetic books. They typically contain the oracles of an individual prophet, although they may also give some details about his life, and in some cases include actual biographical narrative. Moreover, the other prophetic books appear to have been initially composed during or shortly after the prophet's lifetime as a message to his contemporaries. The book of Jonah, on the other hand, may have been composed well after the prophet lived, with a message intended for a later generation.

Despite all this, because the book's essential message is about how the people of Israel can fulfill their unique role within God's purposes in salvation history, a good argument can still be made that the best place to locate this special case is among prophets. That's the focus of their message as well. But we should still be aware of the particular challenges that the book of Jonah presents for interpretation. Even if it's grouped with the other prophetic books, this shouldn't keep us from realizing that it's a different kind of writing and that we need to approach it differently.

In short, we shouldn't uncritically embrace the expectations that the traditional order creates regarding when or why a given book was written, or what kind of writing it is. This is particularly true since the order we're used to reflects only the current state of a tradition that has varied over time and still varies from place to place. Indeed, to have a fixed sequence at all is a more recent development. For the first three-quarters of the Bible's history, its books were presented in a great variety of orders.

Roger Beckwith notes that in the case of the Old Testament, "This stability of order is a relatively modern phenomenon, and owes a good deal to the invention of printing. It was preceded by an era of fluidity, both among the Jews (the chief guardians of the Hebrew Bible) and among Christians (the chief guardians of the Greek)."[16] Beckwith notes seventy-nine different attested orders for the books of the Old Testament. These orders were developed as various liturgical, historical, and literary goals were pursued. There are some general constants: the "five books of Moses," for example, are nearly always kept together, as they should be, since they are they simply the parts into which the Torah has been divided. (In one case, however, the sequence is Genesis, Exodus, Leviticus,

Joshua, Deuteronomy, Numbers.) The books of Joshua, Judges, Samuel, and Kings nearly always appear in this order (although in one case Jeremiah comes between Samuel and Kings, and Ruth is often attached to Judges). But the other books of the Old Testament have been presented in many different sequences.

For the major prophets, the following orders are attested (with Lamentations sometimes appended to Jeremiah):

Isaiah—Jeremiah—Ezekiel

Isaiah—Ezekiel—Jeremiah

Jeremiah—Isaiah—Ezekiel

Jeremiah—Ezekiel—Isaiah

Ezekiel—Isaiah—Jeremiah

The minor prophets generally follow the major prophets in Hebrew manuscripts, but they come before them in many manuscripts of the Septuagint (Greek Old Testament). And in the Septuagint the first six minor prophets appear in this order: Hosea, Amos, Micah, Joel, Obadiah, Jonah. The order that's customary in English Bibles is rather: Hosea, Joel, Amos, Obadiah, Jonah, Micah.

The group of Old Testament books known as the "Writings" appear in an even greater variety of orders than the prophets. In the tradition reflected in historic Christian Bibles, they're not even kept together consistently as a group. Job, for example, is put right after the Pentateuch in several cases. Chronicles can be placed after Samuel–Kings. Ruth, as we've already seen, is sometimes attached to Judges, and Lamentations can be treated as part of Jeremiah.

The books of the New Testament also appear historically in a variety of orders. Bruce Metzger observes that these books are typically gathered into five groups, in this sequence: the gospels; Acts; Paul's epistles; the general epistles; and Revelation. But Metzger then notes, "Prior to the invention of printing, however, there were many other sequences, not only of the five main groups of books, but also of the several books within each group."[17] While the gospels, for example, are always kept together, they are found in nine different sequences, including two in which Luke is placed last and followed immediately by Acts, possibly out of a desire to keep the two volumes of this historical study together. Acts usually follows the gospels, although in three cases the Pauline epistles come between the gospels and Acts, and Acts can also be found after both the Pauline and the general epistles.[18]

And while we're used to encountering the general epistles after Paul's letters, Metzger notes that "virtually all Greek manuscripts of the New Testament place [them] . . . before the Pauline Epistles."[19] Paul's letters themselves appear in seventeen different sequences. Hebrews is typically placed at the end of them, but in various manuscripts it's inserted among them, in a number of different places: after Romans, 2 Corinthians, Galatians, or 2 Thessalonians. The general epistles are found in seven different orders, including one that seems to be determined by the number of epistles each author wrote: John (3), Peter (2), Jude (1), James (1). A sequence in which the book of Revelation follows the gospels, instead of concluding the entire New Testament, is attested several times.[20]

Metzger concludes that "the very great variety in order, both of the several parts of the New Testament as well as of books within each part, leads one to conclude that such matters were of no great significance for the ancient and medieval Church; they became an issue only with later editors and publishers."[21] The advent of printing caused the order of the books of the Bible to become greatly standardized. Nevertheless, because of the way this order had already varied over time, at least four different "established" orders are now in use today: one by Protestants and Catholics;[22] one by Greek Orthodox Christians; one by Syrian Orthodox Christians; and one by Jews, for the Hebrew Scriptures. For that matter, various modern editions of the Bible have presented the books in other sequences. Any book order we might be familiar with and even take for granted really only reflects the current state of a tradition that was fluid for much of its history and still varies today. This is all the more reason not to accept interpretations suggested by book order that keep us from appreciating the true character of literary compositions within the Bible.

The *titles* of the books of the Bible are a final aspect of its historical reshaping that can interfere with our understanding. While the biblical books bear titles that in many cases are very ancient, none of them are original. That is, they weren't chosen by the authors. Others assigned these titles later. Some of them have changed significantly over time, and even today certain books of the Bible are known by different titles in different places. In other words, like the customary book sequence, the book titles we're familiar with simply represent the way the Bible has been shaped over time and from culture to culture.

In the Hebrew Bible, titles were typically given to individual books that either referred to their authors or main characters (e.g. Jeremiah, Ruth) or else were descriptive of their content (Psalms, for example, was called *Tehillim*, "praises"). But the Torah was treated differently. As we've noted, its five "books" are really parts of a unified whole, and so their opening words were used to describe them instead. The book we know as Genesis was called *Bereshith*, "In the Beginning." Exodus was referred to as *Shemoth*, "Names," since this book begins, "These are the names of the sons of Israel who went to Egypt with Jacob." And so on.[23]

Some of these first-line titles were originally longer than the ones used today. Origen wrote around AD 240 in his commentary on Psalms that the Jews of his day called Exodus *Welesmoth*.[24] This was an abbreviation of *w'elleh shemoth*, "These are the names," but it was a longer abbreviation than *Shemoth*, the name Jews use for this book today. Origen also notes that Deuteronomy was called *Eleaddebareim*, from the book's opening *'elleh haddebarim*, "These are the words" (the ones Moses spoke to all Israel). Jews now call this book simply *Debarim*, "words."

When the Old Testament was translated into Greek, its books were given titles that were, for the most part, simply translations into Greek of their traditional Hebrew titles. *Shoftim*, for example, became *Kritai*; both words mean "Judges." *Qoholeth* ("preacher") was translated as *Ecclesiastes*. When the Hebrew titles were proper names, Greek forms were used, so that *Tsephanyah* (Zephaniah) became *Sophonias*. But in some cases the titles were actually changed. The five books of the Torah were no longer described by their opening words, but given Greek titles intended to reflect their content. *Bereshith* thus became *Genesis* ("beginning" or "origin"), *Shemoth* became *Exodus* ("going out"), and so on. Some books were known by a few different names at first: *Exodus* was also called *Exagoge* ("leading out"); *Deuteronomy* ("second law") was also known as *Epinomis* ("after-law") or as the *Protreptika* or *Paraineseis* ("exhortations"). Judges was also called "Judgements," and Psalms was sometimes known as "Hymns."[25]

Some other books were given new Greek names that reflected a different understanding of their content from the one suggested by their Hebrew titles. The Jews called the book of Chronicles, for example, *Dibre ha-yomim*, literally "words of the days," describing a regularly-kept record of events. But in Greek this book was retitled *Paralipomenon*, meaning "things left aside," "leftovers," or "omissions." This was a reference to the significant amount of material the book contained that was not in Samuel–Kings. And those books, for their part, were each retitled *Basileion*: "Kingdoms" or "Reigns." (As I noted above, these works were divided when they were translated, resulting in a First and Second *Paralipomenon* and First through Fourth Reigns.)

The New Testament books, for their part, were also not named by their authors. Their titles too came from those who copied and collected them. Most of the New Testament books are letters, and these were named after either their authors or their recipients. The gospels were named after their presumed authors, while the *Praxeis Apostolon* (Acts of the Apostles) was named after its main characters and the *Apocalypsis Ioannou* (Revelation of John) was named after its author.

Some further changes to the titles of the biblical books were made in the Vulgate, Jerome's influential Latin translation of the Bible, which he completed near the end of the fourth century. For the most part Jerome adopted the traditional Greek titles and simply translated them into Latin, so that *Arithmoi* became *Numeri* ("Numbers"); *Kritai* became the *Liber Iudicum* ("Book of Judges"); and *Paroimiai* became *Liber Proverbiorum* ("Book of Proverbs"). Proper names that served as book titles appeared in Latinized forms in the Vulgate. But instead of translating the titles of some books, Jerome transliterated them. That is, he carried them over letter-for-letter from the Greek. Transliterated titles included Genesis, Exodus, Leviticus, Deuteronomy, Psalms, Ecclesiastes, and *Paralipomenon*. Finally, aware that the books that were known in Greek as First through Fourth Reigns had originally been entitled Samuel and Kings in Hebrew, Jerome provided a double name for each of these books. He used the term "Kings" instead of "Reigns," and so called the first two books both 1–2 Samuel and 1–2 Kings, and the next two both 1–2 Kings and 3–4 Kings.

Finally, when the Bible was translated into the common languages of Europe, most of these titles from the
Latin version were adopted. Typically this was through
translation (so that *Canticum canticorum*, for example,
became the Song of Songs in English). But sometimes it
was once again through transliteration, so that Greek titles
like Genesis and Ecclesiastes found their way from Greek
through Latin into English and other languages. And one
of the books had its title changed back to something closer
in meaning to its traditional Hebrew title. Martin Luther
was aware that while Jerome had retained the Greek title
Paralipomenon in the Vulgate, he had also commented that
the book could be called "more clearly a *chronicle* of all
of Divine history."[26] Luther adopted this suggestion, using
the name *die Chronika* in his German Bible. His example
was soon followed in other European languages. Hence
we today know this book, in the two parts into which it
has been divided, as First and Second Chronicles, under
the "new" name it was given during the Reformation after
going by *Paralipomenon* in Greek and Latin Bibles for well
over fifteen hundred years.

Luther also changed some other titles. Rather than continue to transliterate the Greek word *Ecclesiastes* as Jerome
had done, he translated the Hebrew *Qoholeth* as *Prediger*
("Preacher"). Rather than offer a word-for-word translation
of the Hebrew title *Shir ha-Shirim* ("Song of Songs"), he
translated the meaning of the phrase, entitling this book
the *Hohelied* or "High Song," meaning the "best song." And
he called the Acts of the Apostles the *Apostelgeschichte,* or
"history of the apostles."

Various biblical books have thus had their titles changed in a number of ways over the centuries. The titles that have changed the least are the ones based on proper names. But many of these have altered quite a bit as they've moved from one language to another (from *Tsephanyah* to *Sophonias* to Zephaniah, for example). Other titles have changed more significantly. Books that were originally known by their first lines in Hebrew (the books of the Pentateuch, and Lamentations[27]) were given Greek titles that described their contents instead. And some titles that already were descriptive were changed to reflect a different understanding of a book's contents. Finally, the titles of some books were transliterated instead of being translated; as a result, they ceased to be a meaningful description of the book in the new language and became simply a proper name. Some books have actually undergone two or more of these kinds of changes. Deuteronomy, for example, was originally known by its first line in Hebrew; it was then given a content-descriptive title in Greek; and it's now known by a transliteration of that title that functions basically as a proper name.

Even now some biblical books are known by different titles in different contexts. The King James Version follows Jerome's example of giving two different names for the books that Samuel and Kings were divided into. It refers, for instance, to "The First Book of Samuel, Otherwise Called, the First Book of the Kings." Song of Songs is known in many English versions as Song of Solomon.

In light of this survey, it should be clear that the biblical book titles we're familiar with simply reflect the way the

Bible has been reshaped as it's moved from one culture to another. These titles have changed less than the book order has. Book order varied significantly until the invention of printing in the fifteenth century, while the book titles we know are essentially derived from the fourth-century Vulgate. (In English Bibles, however, Anglo-Saxon terms have been used in place of Latin ones in some cases, and *Paralipomenon* has become Chronicles.) Despite this essential continuity for so many centuries, we must recognize that these book titles are not necessarily a reliable indication of content or message.

How is our understanding of the books of the Bible affected by their traditional titles? Let's consider, to begin with, the matter of *authorship*. The cultural reshaping of the Bible has had a tendency to attribute anonymous books to known figures. None of the five songs in the book of Lamentations, for example, are ascribed to anyone. In the Septuagint, however, this book was given the title "The Lamentations of Jeremiah," and its association with that prophet continues to this day. Its traditional placement right after Jeremiah reinforces this association. (Lamentations has sometimes even been treated as part of that book.) Jeremiah may have been considered the author because we're told near the end of Chronicles that he "composed laments for Josiah" when that king was killed in battle. It's certainly plausible that Jeremiah might also have written laments twenty-three years later, when Jerusalem was destroyed. But in order to approach Lamentations on its own terms, we need to be open to the possibility that its songs were actually written by someone else, who didn't live in Jeremiah's time.

To give another example, the book we know as the "Gospel of Matthew" is also anonymous—the author isn't identified anywhere within its pages. If we're influenced by the traditional title, we'll read this book as if it had been written by someone who lived in Palestine and was a contemporary of Jesus. But there are many indications within the book that it may have been written a generation later, by someone who lived outside of Palestine. We shouldn't let the traditional title keep us from recognizing this possibility and seeing how it can help us understand the book.

Some editions of the Bible assign even more books to well-known figures. For example, the King James Version (KJV) gives Hebrews the title, "The Epistle of Paul the Apostle to the Hebrews." But if we truly want to understand this book, we shouldn't begin with the assumption that Paul wrote it. There are many indications that someone else wrote it instead. The author of Hebrews says he heard about Jesus from others, while Paul insists he met Jesus personally. Hebrews is written to Jewish believers to argue that a new covenant has replaced the old one, while Paul generally speaks more appreciatively of the old covenant, as containing promises that include Gentiles as well as the Jews. (For example, "If you belong to Christ, then you are Abraham's seed, and heirs according to the promise.") For Paul the "true temple" is the Christian community, where God now dwells by the Spirit; for the author of Hebrews, the "true temple" is the heavenly one that provided a model for the earthly tabernacle. In short, while Hebrews doesn't contradict Paul's teaching, it's complementary to it, not identical with it. So we shouldn't let the book's title in the KJV lead us to read Hebrews as if it were saying all the same things Paul does.

The KJV also uses the title "The Revelation of St. John the Divine," attributing that book to the same author as the Gospel of John. But we shouldn't let this title keep us from recognizing that Revelation comes from a very different stream within early Christianity than John's gospel does. This makes it unlikely that the same person was responsible for both books. Indeed, the fact that the author of Revelation identifies himself as "John" suggests he wasn't the same person who wrote the Gospel of John. That book's author doesn't write in his own name, but identifies himself only as "the disciple whom Jesus loved." It may still be inferred from the text of this gospel that its author was the apostle John. But if he didn't want identify himself by name there (or in any of his three epistles), why would he have done so in the book of Revelation?

So we shouldn't consider the traditional titles a reliable indication of a book's *author* in every case. We should also be careful not to allow these titles to create the wrong assumptions about the *intended audience* of a biblical book. The book of Ephesians, in the form we know it today, is addressed to "God's holy people in Ephesus." However, the phrase "in Ephesus" is not found in several early and important manuscripts, and so this phrase may be a later addition. There are suggestions within the epistle itself that Paul is writing to a group of believers he's never met: he tells them that he's "heard about" their faith, and says later that they've no doubt "heard about" him too. Paul would hardly write this to the Ephesians, because he lived with them for two years. Paul doesn't include any greetings in this letter, as he would if he were writing to his old friends in Ephesus. And so this book may actually be the letter to the Laodiceans that's mentioned at the end of Colossians or else a circular letter Paul sent to a group of churches in Asia Minor.

The traditional titles can also mislead us with regard to a book's *central focus*. We saw earlier that the name Genesis is derived from a Greek word meaning "beginnings" or "origins." This name might lead us to believe that the purpose of the book of Genesis is to tell us how everything got here. But this book is really much more about the series of covenants God made with humanity than the physical origins of the universe. We may be looking with such interest throughout the book for the "how" of origins that we miss this covenantal emphasis entirely.

In the same way, we would expect a book with a title of "Exodus" to describe a group's departure from a place, and this book indeed describes how the Israelites came out of Egypt. But it has much more to say about the covenant at Sinai and the construction of the tabernacle than about this "exodus." Nevertheless, because of its title, we might be tempted to conclude we've finished with main business of the book after we've read only the first third of it.

Book titles can also lead us to have the wrong expectations of a book's *genre*. The book of James begins as a letter would, and so it is customarily entitled "the epistle of James." However, as we noted above, this book actually has very strong affinities to works of wisdom literature such as Proverbs. It presents a series of pithy sayings and brief reflections on the human condition. It doesn't develop logically and systematically, the way an epistle would. And so we shouldn't try to read this book the way we would read an ordinary epistle.

In summary, the familiar titles of the biblical books are yet another aspect of the Bible's cultural reshaping on the book level that can interfere with our understanding. These titles can misrepresent the contents and emphases of books, and they can encourage wrong assumptions about who wrote them and why and what kind of writing they are.

We should still approach the Bible on the book level, as a collection of literary creations. But we do need to be aware of how the boundaries, order, and titles we're accustomed to can keep us from engaging the real biblical books on their own terms. None of these elements are original. They simply reflect the current state of a tradition that has varied significantly over time, and which still varies from place to place. We shouldn't allow them to continue governing our interpretations. In our approach to the Bible, we need to be informed and guided instead by the internal structures and emphases of the biblical books as literary compositions. Only this will give the Bible's stories, songs, poems, and dreams their voice back and allow them to speak afresh to a generation that won't be able to hear God's word otherwise.

Chapter Three
A Bible without Chapters & Verses

The need for new presentations of the Bible began to make itself felt keenly in the late 1990s and the early years of our new century. Publishers, demographers, and literacy advocates who were conducting research on Bible reading discovered that while millions of Bibles were being distributed in North America every year, relatively few of them were ever read.

Some of the reasons why people weren't reading the Bible reflected larger social trends. In a post-Christian society, people were much less likely to hear the Bible being read aloud, quoted, or used in illustrations. So it was an unfamiliar book. Moreover, the late-modern worldview, which embraced pluralism and relativism and was skeptical of absolute truth claims, made people wary of a book that claimed to be the word of God.

But there was also a much more practical reason why people weren't reading the Bible. Even when they did open its covers, what they found inside was like no other book they'd ever seen. The text was set in narrow double columns and sprinkled liberally with large and small numbers (indicating chapters and verses) and italicized letters (signaling footnotes). Newer, younger readers found this format particularly confusing and uninviting. The "supremely great literature" that could have drawn them in was still there, but it was masked. As a result, all the work that had to be done just to get them to pick up a Bible was being wasted.

Even those who were already believers, who felt that they should read the Bible and wanted to, often reported that their experience with Scripture was spiritually dry and unsatisfying. It didn't keep them coming back for more. It wasn't surprising, then, that in the United States, while over 90 percent of homes had a Bible, it was only being read with any degree of regularity in 15 percent of them.

This research was of particular concern to Glenn Paauw, director of product development for the U.S. division of the International Bible Society (IBS, now Biblica). Glenn began to reflect on what he and his team could do to encourage more and better Bible reading. IBS was committed to "Scripture-based evangelism" because they believed the Bible is the inspired word of God and has inherent power to bring people to salvation and transform their lives. "Success" for an organization with IBS's mission couldn't be measured simply by the numbers of Bibles being printed and distributed if those Bibles weren't being read and lives weren't being changed.

Glenn recognized that some of the reasons why people weren't reading the Bible couldn't be addressed by publishers alone. But he also knew that in his position, he could at least work to present the Bible in a more appealing and accessible form. And so he began to ask, "In what different format could the Bible be offered to people who are not reading it, to encourage them to begin reading? What changes in presentation would help current readers engage the Bible with greater understanding and satisfaction?"

The *People of the Book* series, produced by IBS under Glenn's direction, represented an early expression of this vision. In separate volumes published from 2000 through 2003, this series used Scripture text printed without chapter or verse numbers to tell the life stories of individual biblical characters, specifically David; Moses; Abraham, Isaac, and Jacob; women of the Old Testament; and Jesus. These stories were divided into "chapters" of their own that corresponded to major episodes and periods in the characters' lives. The volume dedicated to Jesus in the *People of the Book* series consisted of the entire gospel of Luke. It was thus an individually bound "book of the Bible" that was organized according to its own episodes rather than by the traditional chapter-and-verse system.

Another early effort from Glenn's department was the *Encountering Jesus Journal* (2003), which presented selections from the gospels with no numbers in the text. An *Encountering Jesus New Testament* was developed over the next two years using the same format as the journal.

In 2003, Glenn put together a project team to develop a new format for the whole Bible that could help today's readers appreciate and understand the word of God better on its own terms. For this team he drew on the capable staff of his own department, which included (at various times during the four years that this edition was being developed) editors Lisa Anderson, Paul Berry, John Dunham, Jim Rottenborn, and Micah Wierenga. Glenn also engaged some consultants. One of these was John Kohlenberger, president of Blue Heron Bookcraft (a major Bible typesetter) and author or editor of some three dozen Bible reference works. John had been a pioneer in the application of computers to the production of Bible reference works such as concordances. A second consultant was Dr. Gene Rubingh, who had recently retired after thirteen years as vice president for translation at IBS. During those years he coordinated the work of seventy Bible translation teams around the world, training them in translation techniques, cross-cultural communication, and hermeneutics (the application of biblical principles to specific cultures).

Glenn invited me to be a consultant as well when he learned of the research, writing, and teaching I was doing on "the Bible without chapters and verses." I was using this phrase to warn against the distortions that occur in our interpretations when we treat chapters and verses as intentional units. I was also speaking of "the Bible without chapters and verses" to encourage people to read the Scriptures as a collection of literary creations: to seek to understand who wrote them, and for what reason; what kind of writing they were; how they were put together; and what their central message was. These were concepts I'd been pursuing in relation to the biblical books ever since my undergraduate studies in literature at Harvard. I investigated them further in seminary at Gordon-Conwell and in my doctoral program at Boston College, where I studied and later published on the internally-indicated literary structures of several biblical books.[1] In my work as a pastor in the years that followed, as I led Bible studies and adult classes and preached expository sermon series, I had the opportunity to teach through many more books, always with a view toward understanding their inherent designs and presenting them as whole literary works. I consolidated my research and reflections when I taught a course on "The Bible Without Chapters and Verses" at the 1999 Regent College Summer School. Afterward I wrote up my lectures and made them available on the Internet. When Glenn saw them there (thanks to a referral by a mutual friend), he realized that I shared his vision for a new format of the Bible that would allow its literary beauties and theological truths to shine forth unimpeded by the cultural reshaping that has obscured them.

Thus the project team, which came to be known as the Bible Design Group, was formed. Starting in September 2003, our group held working meetings about every other month for a year and a half, with members pursuing individual assignments in between.

Our work together was informed by a variety of resources. These included several earlier editions, such as *The Modern Reader's Bible* and *The Bible Designed to*

For a much fuller description of how various English Bibles since 1700 have tried to minimize the effects of chapters and verses and the order, boundaries, and titles of the biblical books, visit www.thebooksofthebible.info/1700.

Be Read as Living Literature,[2] that had taken various steps toward removing chapters and verses and highlighting the literary compositions within the Scriptures. These editions helped us both theoretically, through the discussions in their introductions, and practically, through the formatting approaches they illustrated. We also consulted a wide range of scholarly books, commentaries, and articles. These helped inform our eventual decisions about the placement and presentation of individual works within the Bible.

But there were also some references that were particularly helpful in guiding our thinking about what overall approach to take. Among these were *The Literary Guide to the Bible*, an anthology of scholarly articles edited by Robert Alter and Frank Kermode; *The New Testament in its Literary Environment* by David Aune; and *How to Read the Bible Book by Book* by Gordon Fee and Douglas Stuart (which appeared shortly before our group first convened).[3] A number of articles also helped shape our strategic thinking, such as "The Greatest Story Never Read" by Gary M. Burge[4] and "Bible Stories for Derrida's Children: Literary Approaches to a Sacred Book" by Leland Ryken.[5]

In his article, Ryken described three different approaches that could be taken to formatting the Bible. "One," he wrote, "is to allow the Bible to remain what it is for most readers—a collection of relatively self-contained units, with individual passages experienced mainly as daily devotional readings or the basis of Sunday sermons." We already knew that the fragmentation of the Scriptures by chapters and verses into "self-contained units" kept people from reading with greater enjoyment and understanding.

So this was definitely not an option. Ryken observed that a second approach was to "smooth out the rough places, and by selectivity and a uniform prose style make the Bible a continuous narrative." This, we realized, was one example of how a publisher might recast the Bible into a contemporary literary form. But this would "bring it to the readers" and allow them to engage the Bible on their terms, rather than "bringing the readers to it" and encouraging them to engage the Bible on its own terms. We acknowledged that it might be helpful to recast the Scriptures into a contemporary literary form if this would at least make people more familiar and comfortable with the Bible's content. This approach has already been taken in various ways. But we recognized that presentations like these don't give readers a full engagement with literary creations that actually make up the Scriptures. We therefore identified most strongly with the third approach Ryken described: "to accept the diversity and ancientness of the [biblical] anthology as it has come to us but to give readers the critical tools of analysis and interpretation that will equip them to cope with individual texts and the book as a whole."[6] Ryken's description of these contrasting approaches helped us recognize the course we wanted to follow. We weren't going to leave the Bible looking like a "collection of relatively self-contained units." And we weren't going to turn the Bible into a contemporary kind of writing. Instead, we would try to present this collection of ancient writings in a way that would make them much more accessible to contemporary readers. The title we eventually chose for our edition expressed this vision: *The Books of The Bible*.

During our year and a half of regular meetings, we developed a good idea of what the new format's main features might be. One of our first decisions, agreed upon with little debate, was to set the Bible in a single column and to remove chapter and verse numbers from the text. We recognized that chapters and verses reflected the modern reshaping of the Bible, that they typically suggested the wrong divisions within biblical books, and that they encouraged disintegrative habits of reading. We didn't even want to move these numbers to the margins, where readers might still think they should be used for navigation. We wouldn't have been opposed, in fact, to removing them from the page entirely. But we recognized it would be prudent to allow current readers of the Bible to orient themselves by reference to a system they were already familiar with, and so we decided to place a chapter-and-verse range, in lighter type, at the bottom of each page.

An early decision was also reached to represent the internal divisions of the biblical books without inserting any descriptive headings or other marks. We admired how easy it was to read editions that used unobtrusive printing conventions like *The Twentieth Century New Testament*,[7] where just a blank line was used to show literary divisions smaller than those indicated by headings, or Richmond Lattimore's translation of the New Testament,[8] which used blank lines alone. We ultimately decided to use only white space of varying widths to indicate the biblical books' literary designs. Following the principle of "the higher the division, the wider the space," we used up to four lines in places to indicate the structures of complex books.

(It's one thing to ask how the natural structure of a biblical book might best be *indicated* by a publisher; it's another matter to ask how this structure can be *identified* in the first place. Identifying biblical book structures was one of my primary responsibilities as part of the Bible Design Group. I'll explain at the end of this chapter how I went about it. Because I'd like to offer a detailed explanation, I won't interrupt the story of how *The Books of The Bible* was developed to give it here.)

The full Bible in Today's New International Version (TNIV) was completed by the Committee on Bible Translation (CBT) and published early in 2005. Because IBS was the copyright holder of the TNIV, our group would have the privilege of using this state-of-the-art translation for the new format we were developing. (*The Books of The Bible* will be available in the NIV when it is updated in 2011.)

The TNIV includes italicized sectional headings throughout, "as an aid to the reader." The translators specify in their preface, however, that these headings "are not to be regarded as part of the biblical text."[9] TNIV Bibles may be published without them, and it seemed consistent with our overall purposes not to include these headings in our planned edition. We found that when the text was set in a single column without chapter and verse numbers or headings, the distinctive ways in which the CBT translators had already represented different literary genres became much more evident. This was visual confirmation for us that chapter and verse divisions, when present, unfortunately do make all the biblical books look like the same kind of writing. But setting the text in this new way also revealed that the Bible, when freed from this modern reshaping, displays a variety of beautiful and intricate literary forms. As the TNIV's formatting came to prominence, stories and songs, poems and proverbs, letters and lists filled the pages of the Bible in a way we hadn't seen before.

The TNIV includes hundreds of notes that clarify terms, provide alternative translations and textual readings, supply modern equivalents of ancient weights and measures, and identify the sources of quotations. We recognized that these notes were an essential part of the translation itself and that it was very important for them to be available to readers. At the same time, however, we felt that printing them at the bottom of the page and signaling them within the text by italicized letters would interrupt the continuous reading we wanted to encourage. We eventually decided to present endnotes after each book, identified by callout phrases, and to signal them subtly within the text with a small raised circle shaded in lighter type.[10]

The creation of endnotes was one specific expression of a general decision we reached early in our discussions: to place all supporting materials outside the actual text of biblical books. We often drew an analogy to the DVD, which allows viewers to access and watch a film by itself, in its entirety, and then separately call up features such as "making of" documentary shorts, interviews with cast and crew, and music videos. We resolved to present the biblical books uninterrupted as whole literary works, but also to provide explanatory "features" outside them in the form of book and section introductions and endnotes. We envisioned even these materials being surrounded by a further layer of information and instruction as people read and discussed the Bible together and shared their insights. We expressed this idea in our preface to the edition: "we encourage readers to study the Bible in community, because we believe that if they do, they, their teachers, leaders and peers will provide one another with much more information and many more insights than could ever be included between the covers of a printed Bible."[11]

We reached decisions on these questions of formatting and presentation early in our discussions. It took many more months to settle on approaches to the boundaries, order, and titles of the biblical books.

In the case of book boundaries, we ultimately concluded that we should recombine Samuel–Kings, Chronicles–Ezra–Nehemiah and Luke–Acts into single books. We might similarly have recombined the five parts of the Torah, but we wanted readers to be able to recognize the way some later biblical writings allude to this fivefold division in their literary shapes. We considered these allusions significant for interpretation, so we left Genesis through Deuteronomy as separate books. But we wrote a single introduction to Exodus, Leviticus, and Numbers, to highlight the way they are tied together by a single structural pattern. (We also wrote a single introduction Joshua and Judges, which are closely integrated books.) Thus we presented the full contents of the canon in fifty-nine books rather than the traditional sixty-six.

In terms of book names, we concluded after much discussion that the challenge for interpretation presented by the traditional titles of the books of the Bible could best be met by an approach that:

(1) provided enough continuity with the tradition to allow readers who already had some familiarity with the Bible to recognize books;

(2) didn't perpetuate the interpretations of authorship, audience, and genre suggested by the traditional titles; and

(3) didn't simply substitute alternative interpretations for these, but allowed readers to consider a range of possibilities.

We therefore decided to use the abbreviated titles now employed by many publishers as a kind of shorthand to identify books in a familiar way, without necessarily suggesting that these titles were descriptive of genre, authorship, or audience. Thus we used the titles such as James and Acts rather than "The Epistle of James" or "The Acts of the Apostles"; Matthew instead of "The Gospel According to St. Matthew"; and Ephesians in place of "The Letter of Paul to the Ephesians."

The question of book order generated some of our most extensive discussions. We knew there were numerous historical precedents for putting the biblical books in various orders, depending on the goals of a presentation. In preparing *The Books of The Bible*, our goal was to help today's readers engage the Scriptures with greater understanding and enjoyment. We wanted to put the biblical books in an order that would help overcome the difficulties the traditional sequence can create. We didn't want people to keep getting the wrong expectations about genre, or to have difficulty appreciating why and when certain books were written. And so we tried to group books together that came from the same broad stream within the believing community, or that were the same kind of writing. (We were sometimes able to use these two considerations together. They both applied to the books in the prophetic and wisdom traditions, for example.) Secondarily, within these groups of books, we used chronological order to help readers further appreciate books' historical settings.

This meant specifically, in the case of the First Testament (the Old Testament), presenting the books in three main divisions. As our introduction to the First Testament in *The Books of The Bible* explains:

> The first division, Covenant History, includes not just the books that the Hebrews call the "law" (Genesis–Deuteronomy), but also the books they call the "former prophets" (Joshua–Kings), since all of these books together make up a continuous narrative. It tells the story of God's dealings with humanity from the beginning of the world up to the time when the people of Israel were conquered and sent into exile. The second division presents the books that the Hebrews call the "latter prophets." While these are traditionally divided into two groups according to their size (the long books being considered the "major prophets" and the short ones the "minor prophets"), here they are presented together in what we believe to be their historical order. The third division contains the "writings." These are grouped according to what kind of literature they are: song lyrics, wisdom, history or apocalypse.[12]

In the New Testament, we grouped together works that seemed to come from the same broad stream within the first-century community of Christ's followers. We then worked out what we felt was an appropriate order for these groups. As we put it in the introduction to the New Testament in *The Books of The Bible*:

> We have reunited the two volumes of Luke–Acts and placed them first because they provide an overview of the New Testament period. This allows readers to see where most of the other books belong. Next come Paul's letters in the order in which we believe they were most likely written. Luke was one of Paul's co-workers in sharing the good news about Jesus, so his volumes are well suited to accompany Paul's letters. The gospel according to Matthew comes next, together with two books, Hebrews and James, also addressed to Jews who believed in Jesus as their Messiah. Then comes the gospel according to Mark (which many scholars believe was actually the first gospel to be written), together with the letters of Peter, since Mark seems to tell the story of Jesus' life from Peter's perspective. Also included in this group is the letter of Jude, which has many similarities with Peter's second letter. Our final group begins with the gospel according to John, which can suitably come last among the gospels because it represents a mature reflection, after many years, on the meaning of Jesus' life. The letters of John follow his gospel.

The book of Revelation is appropriately placed last and by itself, since it is unique in literary type and perspective, and it describes how God's saving plan for all of creation will ultimately be realized.[13]

We were delighted to discover that through this presentation, we were able to "express the ancient concept of the fourfold gospel in a fresh way." In this arrangement,

The traditional priority of the stories of Jesus is retained, but now each gospel is placed at the beginning of a group of related books. Thus the presentation of four witnesses to the one gospel of Jesus the Messiah is enhanced by a fuller arrangement that will help readers better appreciate why the books of the New Testament were written and what kind of literature they represent.[14]

By the end of our first year of deliberations, we'd settled on the basic details of the format we were developing. We knew it was time to share our thinking and ideas with IBS's ministry partners and get the benefit of their insights.

Over the next year and a half, members of the Committee on Bible Translation and leaders of the Bible publishing divisions at Zondervan Corporation (the commercial publisher of the TNIV) very generously shared their perspectives on the developing edition. With the benefit of their comments and questions, we were able to refine the format even further.

A Preview Edition of the New Testament was prepared late in 2005 and distributed to several hundred reviewers. These included seminary professors, pastors and Christian workers, publishers and editors, and interested people from many other walks of life. A small number of reviewers responded that they were already reading and studying the Bible meaningfully in the customary format and so didn't see the need for a change. But the overwhelming majority of those who commented on this Preview Edition expressed an enthusiasm and even an excitement about the difference that being able to engage the text so much more directly made in their experience with the Bible. One reviewer wrote, "I love it . . . I found myself understanding the scripture in a new way, with a fresh lens, and I felt spiritually refreshed as a result. I learn much more through stories being told and, with this new format, I felt the truth of the story come alive for me in new ways." Another reported, "I found from personal reading that I drew connections I hadn't drawn before by being forced to read larger chunks." And yet another reviewer wrote:

> I have been a reader of the Bible for all of my life
> . . . But after reading just a few pages (literally), I
> was amazed at what I had been missing all of these
> years. For example, even though I "knew" that 1
> Corinthians was a letter written by Paul, I didn't
> realize that I wasn't reading it as I would a normal
> letter (until after I read the Preview Edition).
> Suddenly, the contents of the letter made more
> sense—and they fit together.

Such comments were very encouraging, since they suggested that the format changes we had been working on would indeed help foster "more and better Bible reading," as we'd hoped.

Many readers of the Preview Edition offered useful suggestions that we agreed could enhance the presentation even further. The experience of seeing the format in actual print also helped us recognize other improvements that could be made. IBS used the principles developed in the Bible Design Group to publish some individual biblical books in the new format, in advance of the release of a full Bible. These included *The Search* (Ecclesiastes) and *The Journey* (the Gospel of John) in 2005, *Kingdom Come, Kingdom Go* (Luke–Acts) and *The Book of Psalms* in 2006, and *Hear This Word* (Amos) in 2007. As the "WordWrights" in product development crafted each of these publications, they gained valuable experience working in the new format. Everything we learned from creating these publications, and from the suggestions we received, was incorporated into the presentation of the TNIV that was published in 2007 as *The Books of The Bible*. Our hope is that this edition will provide both new and returning readers of the Bible with a fresh, life-transforming encounter with the word of God.

From the reports we've heard over the past three years, this hope is being realized. As I mentioned in the introduction to this book, I've been following what users of *The Books of The Bible* have been saying in a variety of venues about their experiences with it. I've corresponded with them and learned more about how it's being used for reading, studying, preaching, and teaching. In the next four chapters, I'll describe how "Bibles without chapters and verses" like this edition can be used for each of these vital Scripture disciplines. As we change our practices to

make full use of new presentations, we'll help the generations that are currently walking away from the Bible come
back and hear God speaking to them through his word
once again.

Before exploring these new practices, however, I'd
like to explain one more aspect of the work I did for the
Bible Design Group. One of my main assignments was
to identify the natural structures of the biblical books so
we could indicate them in *The Books of The Bible*. I was
given this assignment because over the years I had already
investigated the structures of many individual books. In
the process, I had developed and refined an approach that
I felt could be taken to the books of the Bible in general. I
spent an entire day explaining this approach to our team at
the very start of our work, and they agreed it was a very
promising one to take. They also felt that if we used this
one method consistently to identify structures, rather than
drawing on a variety of sources and methods to determine
the literary structure of various books, this would create a
more harmonious presentation throughout the edition.

In my own individual research and in my work for the
Bible Design Group, I began with an authority commit-
ment: the belief that the Bible is the inspired word of God.
More specifically, I believe that its inspiration rests on the
level of authorial intent, not on the level of plain words that
might be taken to mean a number of things.[15] I therefore
proceeded in the belief that just as we seek to discover
authors' intentions in order to understand the meaning of
individual biblical passages, so our understanding of any

biblical book's structure must also be informed by a search for the author's expressed literary-structural intentions.

The search for indications that the biblical authors may have given us of the outlines of their works has good prospects of success. Ancient writers didn't have the freedom to add spacing and headings that abundant, affordable publishing materials now permit modern authors to use to indicate their outlines. Moreover, in many cases ancient works were intended to be delivered orally, and were written down only for transmission to their recipients. (Note, for example, Paul's admonition to the Colossians: "After this letter has been read to you, see that it is also read in the church of the Laodiceans.") For both of these reasons, it has long seemed reasonable to me that ancient authors would have embedded recognizable literary-structural signals directly within their works.

I became convinced, after many years of research and reflection, that within the pages of the Bible these signals characteristically take the form of recurring phrases that have been placed intentionally at the seams of literary structures. One way of confirming that these phrases are being used to signal structural transitions (and that they're not just favorite expressions that authors like to use) is to recognize how their appearances coincide with structural seams that can be identified more implicitly from other characteristics of a work such as shifts in genre, changes in topic, or progression of plot.

Earlier in this book I've already given several examples of how book structures are indicated by recurring phrases. In Chapter 1, I explained how many of the groups of laws in Leviticus conclude with a standard summary formula, "These are the regulations . . ." The use of this formula makes explicit a structure that can be recognized implicitly from the book's topical ordering principle. And we saw in Chapter 2 that the successive reigns described in Samuel–Kings are introduced or concluded by a standard formula that gives a king's name and age and tells how long he reigned.

But the phrases that biblical authors use to indicate structural transitions may be integrated more directly into their works than this. In Chapter 1, we also saw how variations on the phrase "when Jesus had finished saying these things" come right after each of five long discourses in Matthew. (After the last one the wording is, appropriately, "when Jesus had finished saying *all* these things."[16]) The structural significance of these phrases is confirmed by the way they all occur at transitions between discourse and narrative. But unlike the more obvious summary statements in Leviticus and Samuel–Kings, these are built right into the resuming narrative of the gospel itself.

Examples of other similarly embedded structural indicators may readily be provided from other books of the Bible. A variation of the benediction "Praise be to the LORD, the God of Israel, from everlasting to everlasting, Amen and Amen" occurs between each of the five sections that the book of Psalms has been divided into. These benedictions have come to be treated as the endings of the last psalms in each section; they've even been numbered as the last verse of these psalms, even though in some cases they don't match the rest of the psalm very well. Psalm 89, for example, is a lament that would end quite surprisingly with a burst of praise if the benediction were its real conclusion. But this traditional assimilation of the benedictions into the preceding psalms simply indicates how successfully these structural dividers have been integrated into the liturgical material of the book.

Phrases that signal literary structure have also been worked into the biblical collections of prophetic oracles. The book of Zephaniah has three main parts, which treat different themes: prophecies about the worldwide "day of the LORD," oracles against individual nations, and promises of restoration to Israel. The first part ends, "In the fire of his jealousy the whole earth will be consumed [*be'esh qine'atho te'akel kol-ha'erets*], for he will make a sudden end of all who live on the earth." Even though the second part of the book concerns individual nations, it returns to a worldwide perspective at its very end, and it concludes with a phrase that is repeated almost verbatim from the first part of the book, differing by only one letter: "The whole world will be consumed by the fire of my jealous anger [*be'esh qine'athi te'akel kol-ha'erets*]."

The book of Jeremiah, to cite another example, contains four large collections of materials. The first and the last contain mostly poetic oracles; they come from various times in the prophet's career. The middle two collections consist largely of biographical narratives from the later part of Jeremiah's life. In other words, these collections are different kinds of writing and come from different periods. This distinction within the book, which can already be recognized implicitly by these considerations, seems to be signaled explicitly and intentionally (indeed, self-consciously) by the way each section ends with a reference to Jeremiah's words being written down in a book or on a scroll.[17]

Many more examples could be given. But this is not the place to offer an extensive account of the literary-structural signals I believe the biblical authors have sent us in the pages of their works. (The introductions in *The Books of The Bible* describe recurring phrases and references that occur at the seams of other books besides those described here. In late 2011, Biblica will also publish my book featuring these introductions updated and expanded.) I simply want to explain here that I used a consistent method to identify the literary structures that would be indicated in our edition. When recurring phrases appeared at the boundaries between large units in outlines that could already be discerned from a book's other characteristics (genre, plot, topic, theme, etc.), I took these phrases as a signal from the author or editor about literary structure.

Looking to such signals as guides to literary structure is admittedly not the only possible approach. Indeed, there is an active debate among scholars using a variety of methods as to the larger structures of many biblical books. We in the Bible Design Group recognized that this scholarly conversation was in progress; through the publication of *The Books of The Bible*, we wanted to join it. We feel that the method we used to identify literary structures was very valuable for our purposes. In many cases it confirmed analyses offered by others, and in some instances it pointed the way to what we feel are fruitful avenues for future investigation.

Nevertheless, all of the interpretations we're suggesting by publishing *The Books of The Bible* are being offered to readers and students of the Scriptures in a spirit of exploration. We acknowledge that reading itself is a creative act. Through the publication of this edition, we wish to share the beauty that we have come to see in the literary forms of the biblical books, and thereby to encourage Scripture reading with more enjoyment and understanding. We hope that our observations will be tested critically by scholars and other devoted readers of the Bible. If some other analysis suggests a more reasonable account of the authors' intentions in various places, we will gratefully draw on this analysis to improve our own understanding of the Scriptures. But we do believe, nevertheless, that the method we've used does offer considerable promise in identifying the biblical authors' literary-structural designs, and so we are eager to share the results of our explorations to date.

It's valuable to recognize that while scholarly accounts of the larger structures of individual biblical books do vary, the actual structures identified by individual interpreters are not necessarily as divergent as they might first appear. Even when scholars use different methods and suggest contrasting thematic outlines, in the end they may divide a book into almost the same sections as others do. And because *The Books of The Bible* contains no section headings, its indications of book structure can be accommodated within a broad range of interpretations that are still in conversation with one another. In other words, it's not actually necessary to accept that authors' literary-structural intentions have been reliably identified through recurring phrases, or even to believe that authors have sent any intentional signals within their works at all, in order to be comfortable with the basic outlines of the literary structures we are indicating.

For example, in *How to Read the Bible Book by Book* (a volume that was, as I've noted, a valuable and influential resource for our project), Gordon Fee and Douglas Stuart write that 2 Corinthians is "probably two letters . . . combined into one." That is, they believe it's been created by putting together two letters that Paul wrote on separate occasions. They provide the following outline of its contents:

Salutation and Praise to God (1:1–11)

Explanation of Paul's Change of Plans (1:12–2:13)

Paul, Minister of the New Covenant (2:14–7:4)

The Explanation Renewed (7:5–16)

Have the Collection Ready When I Come (8:1–9:15)

Defense of Paul's Ministry against False Apostles (10:1–13:14)

They suggest that the last section specifically was taken from a different letter from the rest of the book as we now know it.[18]

The introduction in *The Books of The Bible*, by contrast, asserts that 2 Corinthians was composed entirely on a single occasion. In describing its structure, we follow an interpretation that Aída Besançon Spencer and William David Spencer offer in their commentary on the book.

Paul is understood to be addressing the Corinthians from a series of perspectives that correspond to geographic locations:

> Paul narrates this letter not along topics or themes. Rather, he uses a chronological schema and inserts along the way theological truths that these different events teach. In 1:3–11, Paul speaks of the troubles in Asia and what they taught about comfort and suffering. In 1:15–17 he speaks of his plans to go to Macedonia, and the importance of trust and love. In 2:12–13 he moves to Troas, a seaport town in Asia across from Macedonia, and discusses the truths he learned there. In 7:5–7 he has now crossed the Aegean Sea into Macedonia and found Titus. In 8:17 Paul begins to envision future travel south into the province of Achaia. In 10:2 he envisions his entrance into Corinth itself. Second Corinthians might thus be understood as a motion picture or a talk, illustrated by a map of the Mediterranean countries, which is periodically halted to explain what was happening in the participants' minds at each place.[19]

In keeping with this interpretation, the structural transitions in the epistle are considered in *The Books of The Bible* to be signaled by certain of these place references. The following outline is thus marked (using line spacing only; headings are provided here just for descriptive purposes):

Epistolary Opening and Thanksgiving (1:1–7)

Paul in Asia: If I make you sad, who can make me happy? (1:8–2:11)

Paul in Troas: Treasure in earthen vessels
(2:12–7:4)

Paul in Macedonia: Working together again
(7:5–9:15)

Paul in Corinth: Are they servants of Christ? I am
more. (10:1–13:10)

Epistolary Closing (13:11–14)

This account of the book's structure would initially appear to differ significantly from the one offered by Fee and Stuart. This should not be surprising, since it reflects a contrasting interpretation of the book's circumstances of composition. However, upon closer inspection, the differences prove to be quite minor, at least in terms of how the book is divided into sections.

Both outlines acknowledge that 2 Corinthians begins with some standard epistolary conventions. The outlines diverge only in how they treat Paul's transition from these conventions into the epistle proper. *The Books of The Bible* considers the main body of the letter to begin when Paul starts addressing the Corinthians directly ("We do not want you to be uninformed"), while Fee and Stuart believe the main body begins only after Paul's references to prayer and thanksgiving. But this just means that they consider the main body to start one (long) Greek sentence later than we do. In both outlines, the third section of the book is virtually the same; Fee and Stuart once again begin this section one (much shorter) Greek sentence later than we do. Their fourth and fifth sections, if taken together, coincide exactly with the fourth section in our edition. And the only other difference is that we have set off the brief epistolary closing elements as a distinct section, just as both outlines set off the opening ones. In other words, even when interpreted from varying perspectives, this epistle still "reads" very much the same way structurally.

The sections into which George Campbell divided Matthew in his 1778 translation of the gospels provide the basis for another useful comparison. Alexander Campbell used this translation in *The Sacred Writings,* another early "Bible without chapters and verses," and incorporated its section headings into his text.[20] The translator divided this gospel into sixteen parts, based on major events in the narrative:

I The Nativity (1:1–2:23)

II The Immersion (3:1–4:25)

III The Sermon on the Mount (5:1–7:28)

IV Several Miracles (8:1–9:34)

V The Charge to the Apostles (9:35–11:1)

VI The Character of the Times (11:2–12:50)

VII Parables (13:1–53)

VIII The People Twice Fed in the Desert (13:54–16:12)

IX The Transfiguration (16:13–18:35)

X The Rich Man's Application (19:1–20:16)

XI The Entry Into Jerusalem (20:17–22:14)

XII The Character of the Pharisees (22:15–23:39)

XIII The Prophecy on Mount Olivet (24:1–25:46)

XIV The Last Supper (26:1–56)

XV The Crucifixion (26:56–27:56)

XVI The Resurrection (27:52–28:20)

Once again, this outline would appear at first to be very different from the one offered in *The Books of The Bible*. There, following the interpretation I summarized in Chapter 1, Matthew is understood to have at its core (between the genealogy and the passion narrative) five "books," narrative-discourse pairs that each develop a shared theme relating to the kingdom of heaven.

But in this case as well, the two perspectives on literary structure are actually quite harmonious. Significantly, in Campbell's outline, each of the repetitions of the phrase "when Jesus had finished saying these things" comes either at the very end or the very beginning of a section. In other words, he too seems to have considered these phrases to be indicators of literary structure. When his sections are set alongside the units in the interpretation of Matthew's structure that we followed in our edition, the essential similarity of the two outlines becomes evident:

Genealogy + Foundations Narrative	**I + II**
Foundations Discourse	**III**
Mission Narrative	**IV**
Mission Discourse	**V**
Mystery Narrative	**VI**

Mystery Discourse	**VII**
Family Narrative + Family Discourse	**VIII + IX**
Destiny Narrative	**X + XI + XII**
Destiny Discourse	**XIII**
Passion Narrative	**XIV + XV + XVI**

One outline will sometimes put a transitional sentence with what precedes, while the other will include it with what follows, but in terms of overall content, the sections are exact matches. Given such examples, we hope it will be recognized that the structural outlines marked without headings in *The Books of The Bible* actually embrace a broad range of underlying interpretations within the scholarly conversation.

It should be observed further that because *The Books of The Bible* is a presentation of Today's New International Version, the members of the Committee on Bible Translation had already determined how the smaller structures of the biblical books would be represented. These translators divided the text into sentences and paragraphs, and we respected their work in every case. This had an indirect influence on the decisions we made regarding how to represent larger structures, since no interpretations could be followed that would have required placing a break within a sentence or paragraph.

In fact, the work of the Committee reached into higher levels of literary structure in some places. The TNIV includes section headings that are intended as an aid to the reader, but which are not meant to be regarded as part of the biblical text. TNIV Bibles may be published without these headings, but if they are omitted, the translators have specified that at certain points spacing must be left where headings would otherwise appear. Many of these spaces preserve distinctions of genre: they set off legal, lyrical, genealogical, or epistolary material that appears within a larger narrative. But in a few places these spaces express interpretations of macrostructure. Spaces are required, for example, before occurrences of the phrase "this is the account of" that marks off the highest-level literary units in Genesis. Once again, we respected these indications in every instance, so that the collective wisdom of the Committee exerted a further indirect influence on the representation of macrostructure in *The Books of The Bible*. (Nevertheless, it should be specified that this presentation of the TNIV is not the work of the Committee on Bible Translation, but of the Bible Design Group, which is solely responsible for it.)

In the end, as great works of literature, many biblical books may be so complex and beautiful in form as to admit multiple perspectives on their literary structures. We therefore don't want to suggest that the interpretations embodied in *The Books of The Bible* are definitive. But we are convinced that this edition offers a reasonable account of literary structure for each of the biblical books. Interpreters will no doubt continue to disagree on structural details, both small and large. But there should be general agreement that encountering the Bible in a clean, plain text, with reasonable structural outlines subtly suggested, will in any event be more profitable to readers than continuing to use chapters and verses as guides to the Scriptures.

Because we wished to honor the ongoing scholarly conversation about the literary structure of many biblical books, we recognized that in the preparation of our edition we needed to proceed humbly, with an openness to all of the insights that could be obtained from the broader scholarly community. We resolved to be receptive to the comments and even criticisms our edition might attract, and to keep it "evergreen"—always open for future revision. But at the same time, we felt an urgency about our task that made us willing to commit to the interpretations we are presenting now. As we state in the Preface to *The Books of The Bible:*

> Just as the work of Bible translation is never finished, the work of formatting the Bible on the principles described here will never be completed. Advances in the literary interpretation of the biblical books will undoubtedly enable the work we have begun here to be extended and improved in the years ahead. Yet the need to help readers overcome the many obstacles inherent in the Bible's current format is urgent, so we humbly offer the results of our work to those seeking an improved visual presentation of its sacred books.[21]

Now that we've seen how this new presentation of the Bible was created, let's look at some of the ways it's been helping people develop new practices of reading, studying, preaching, and teaching that will enable the rising generations to have a fresh encounter with God through the Scriptures.

Chapter Four

Reading the Bible after Chapters & Verses:
Experiencing Whole Books

I f you ask people who like to read to describe what reading is, they'll tell you it means curling up for hours in a favorite chair or on the couch, losing track of time as you get carried off into another world by a novel, history, or biography, or even by a book or magazine about cars, wildlife, cooking, or current events. This isn't how we usually describe reading when we encourage people to read the Bible. Instead, we teach people that each day they should read a selection of relatively short length (about two thousand words), drawn from one or more biblical books, and then stop.

But reading only short stretches like this is directly contrary to the character of the writings in the Bible. As we saw in Chapters 1 and 2, the Scriptures contain works of greatly varying lengths, and the meaningful units within those works are also of different lengths. Some works can be read in a short period of time, while others will take

longer. And within these longer works, while it's sometimes appropriate to pause, reflect, and then resume, at
other times it's best to read continuously. Reading in short
stretches prevents readers from ever "catching fire." That's
not how you read. It's how you take medication.

So why do we think it's worthwhile for people to take
this daily-dose approach? What do we expect them to get
out of the experience? I believe our current Bible reading
practices do reflect a desire to help people reach two very
worthy goals. Unfortunately, because our practices are so
contrary to the actual character of the Scriptures, most
people never reach those goals.

One goal we try to help people reach is reading all the
way through the Bible. We encourage people to do this
because we believe the Scriptures are the inspired word of
God and that everything in them is therefore valuable for
our growth and development. But for many people, trying
to read through the Bible ends up being something like a
Muslim trying to make the *haj* (pilgrimage) to Mecca—a
strenuous devotional exercise. Because the Scriptures are
an extensive collection of writings in unfamiliar genres that
come from distant places and times, and because the Bible
has also been shaped in ways that distort and interrupt the
natural flow of these writings, trying to read all of it is quite
challenging for most people.

But as a rule, we haven't equipped people to recognize,
appreciate, and enjoy the ancient genres found in the
Scriptures. We haven't explained that they shouldn't expect
to read the same amount of text each day, because the

natural units in the Bible are of different sizes. We haven't taught people how use different styles and strategies to engage different kinds of writing. Instead, we've just devised ways to help people "get through" the arduous task of reading a large volume filled with unfamiliar and confusing text. Most typically, we tell people that if they'd just read for ten or fifteen minutes a day, they could get all the way through the Bible in the course of a single year.

Reading plans are widely available that break up the Scriptural writings into selections to be completed and checked off each day. But these reading plans usually don't respect the natural structures of the biblical books. These plans are almost always based on chapters, which certainly are units of a convenient size for this particular enterprise. Read three a day, and you're done in a year. But chapters are an artificial imposition on the text. They typically don't correspond with its natural divisions. And even in those cases where certain chapter breaks do coincide with the larger seams in a book, so that a group of chapters would be equivalent to one of its major sections, reading plans still don't respect even these groupings.

For example, in Paul's letter to the Romans, the traditional chapters numbered from 9 to 11 comprise a distinct discussion of God's future intentions for Israel. But in one plan, which is designed to take readers through the whole Bible sequentially following the traditional book order, Romans 8–10 is assigned on one day and Romans 11–14 on the next.[1] In another plan, which assigns readings from various biblical genres on different days of the week, Romans 9 and 10 are read on one Sunday and Romans 11 and 12 a week later.[2] In either case, with Paul's discussion broken up this way, it's hard to imagine a reader even recognizing that it's a distinct unit within the book, much less following it.[3] But determined readers, who believe they are doing something that is good for them, might at least "get through it."

A desire to offer selections from various genres on different days is only one reason why a plan might have people move back and forth between two or more books at a time, rather than going straight through one book. Some plans assign readings from more than one book each day because they want to offer selections from both the Old Testament and the New Testament. Other plans organize the events and characters of the Bible into a chronological scheme. One such plan gives this illustration of how it has been organized: "Job lived sometime after the beginning of creation (Genesis 1) but before Abraham was born (Genesis 12). As a result, the Book of Job is integrated into the Book of Genesis" (after Genesis 11).[4] The chronological arrangement also leads this plan to assign readings from Jeremiah and Psalms on one day, Kings and Chronicles the next day, and Habakkuk the following day, before finally returning to Jeremiah.[5]

No matter what the rationale behind it, mixing books together like this makes our reading even more discordant with the natural character of the writings in the Scriptures. It doesn't acknowledge and respect the integrity of whole literary compositions. Instead, it reinforces, on a daily basis, an understanding of the Bible as a disorganized jumble of fragments that need to be arranged properly by someone who knows how to impose order on them from the outside.

What other literature would we ever read like this? When we're really reading a book or an article, we wouldn't think of stopping to pick something else up for a while. We're so drawn in, we can't put it down. The only other artistic expression we engage the way we do the Bible is television, when we're channel surfing. We tend to jump around while watching TV because the programs are broken up by commercials. We don't want to wait through the distraction of the commercials for the program we've been watching to resume, so we find another interesting story to follow in the meantime. If the very same programs were presented without commercial interruption, we prob-ably wouldn't change the channel until they were over. But because programs are interrupted, we try to watch several at once, and usually miss something essential in each one.

Exactly the same thing happens when we break up the Bible into short daily selections. The fragmentation and jumbling wreck our attention span. Those who create daily reading plans, and those who try to follow them, have the best of intentions. But these plans don't work. Most attempts to read through the Bible fail.

There's a second, equally admirable goal that we try to help people reach by reading the Scriptures in short daily installments. We encourage people to cultivate their relationship with God by having a "quiet time" each day. We teach people they can talk to God through prayer, and we tell them they can expect to hear God speaking to them through the Bible. As the children's chorus puts it, "Read your Bible, pray every day, and you'll grow, grow, grow."

As that's stated, it's perfectly true. But what we're encouraging people to do isn't really reading. It's actually a pared-down version of the spiritual discipline known as *lectio divina*. One Catholic writer explains that this practice dates back to the fourth and fifth centuries of the Christian era, to the "desert fathers and mothers whose spirituality consisted primarily of prayerful rumination on biblical texts." The discipline was eventually "legislated and to some extent formalized" by the rules that governed monastic orders, and it has been "adapted by contemporary spiritual teachers for our own times." At its heart is the "slow, leisurely, attentive reading (*lectio*) and re-reading of a biblical text," with the expectation that God will be speaking "in and through" it.[6]

Evangelical Protestants don't describe things in exactly this language. They're more likely to encourage the people in their churches to have a "daily quiet time" than to teach them to engage in regular sessions of *lectio divina*. But they still suggest that believers should approach the Scriptures in the same way: as an instrument for making contact with God.

There's an important difference, however. The practice of *lectio divina* developed within a particular kind of community, where people had been taught how to enter deeply into the presence of God, and individual meditation on the meaning of Scripture was informed by the liturgy and devotions of a community that had shared a common life for generations. To try to teach the same method without

providing supporting resources like these is to invite dis-
appointment. Within an individualistic modern context,
readers are more likely to be looking to the text alone, as
an "object," to become a vehicle for the communication of
spiritual knowledge from beyond. Modernity places a high
premium on knowledge and information, and in its spiritual expressions, it approximates a revived Gnosticism, in
which liberating spiritual truth is imparted directly to the
receptive soul. In the modern view, this doesn't need to
happen in interdependence with the community that now
constitutes the body of Christ on earth, or even through
the actual medium of Scripture itself.

The red-letter Bible, in which the words of Jesus are
distinguished by different-colored ink, provides a visual
analogy to what we lead people to expect in their "quiet
times." As God uses the biblical text as a medium of communication, we suggest, some of the words in the passage
before us will "turn red," so to speak—they'll take on a significance above the others. In fact, they will even acquire a
significance beyond what can be derived from their literary
and historical context, and they'll become a direct personal
word from God to us today. In other words, we approach
the Bible with the expectation that, as *The X-Files* puts
it, "The truth is out there." *Out there*—not "in here," not
worked into the fabric of the Scriptures themselves.

This approach to reading the Bible usually fails too.
People don't hear from beyond. It's not that no one's out
there. It's that the God who really is out there hasn't chosen
to communicate with us in this way.

The best way to appreciate *how* we should expect God to speak to us through the Bible is to acknowledge *what* it actually is. Suppose I go to my father and ask him what he thinks I should do in a given situation. If he replies, "Son, let me tell you a story about something that happened to me when I was your age," I know I should look for his advice in the wisdom of his experience as embodied in the choice of this particular story and the shape he gives it as he relates it. He's chosen to communicate this way because he knows he shouldn't be telling me what to do for the rest of my life. He wants me to grow into a person of wisdom and maturity. His *means* of communication signals to me that I shouldn't expect him just to give me a few words that will solve my problems for that day.

Similarly, by giving us a collection of literary compositions as our sacred writings, God has said to us, "Sons, daughters, let me tell you a story." God communicates in this way so that we won't remain immature spiritually, just following orders, but that instead "we will in all things grow up into . . . Christ," as Paul wrote in Ephesians. Yes, from time to time God does give particular guidance, and sometimes it will come through the medium of Scripture. But we should still understand what God has given us in the Bible: a meaningful story. If we continue to think instead that the Bible is a loose assortment of statements that someone needs to organize, we might figure that God can do some organizing too and pick out one or two good ones for us today. But that's not what the Bible is, and that's not how God speaks to us through it.

So the way we encourage people to "read" in short daily selections has been shaped by two admirable motives: a desire to help people read all the way through the Bible, and a desire to help them invest in their relationship with God. But in both cases, the good intentions are rarely realized because the practice we're teaching isn't suited to the true character of the Scriptures.

Our presentations of the Bible have also shaped our reading practices. Whether a person is following a through-the-Bible plan, using a daily devotional guide, or just making an effort to get into God's word as often as possible, they'll encounter "stop signs" at regular intervals, in the form of big bold chapter numbers and italicized section headings that cut across the text. These say visually, "You've read enough now; you should be experiencing some closure here." And even if a person doesn't have the "sense of an ending," they're likely to stop reading anyway, because they feel they should. One young man shared this experience on his blog:

> Last night I started reading through John. . . . I read through 2 chapters, then thought to myself, "Whoa, 2 chapters. Maybe you should stop. That's pretty good." But I kept reading. I ended up reading 5 chapters and growing more and more frustrated with the tiny little numbers (chapters and verse references) that interrupted and distracted me. So I went and bought [a copy of *The Books of The Bible*].

He concluded, significantly, "Hopefully this Bible turns

into something I can't put down." This young man knew what it really meant to "read": to have a book in your hands you just can't put down. He wanted the Bible to be that kind of book for him, and he recognized that the modern format was standing in his way.

Every time we let chapters, sections, the schedule of an annual plan, or the assignments in a daily devotional guide decide for us where we should stop reading the Bible, we miss an opportunity to become better readers. And if the assigned selections don't correspond with natural literary units, we have one more experience that confirms the impression that you just can't make sense of the Bible.

The conclusion is inescapable: if we want to reintroduce the Scriptures to people in the postmodern generations, we shouldn't encourage them to read the Bible every day in short selections. In fact, we should probably encourage them *not* to read the Bible every day. The kind of "reading" that's interesting, enjoyable, satisfying, and meaningful is done in bursts. A person finds a literary work so engaging and absorbing they can't put it down. They sit with it for hours. And when they're done reading, they want to savor the experience, letting the whole work settle into their hearts and minds. They recall favorite passages, recognize the meaning of symbols, make connections in the plot, and talk with their friends or blog about what they've read. In other words, there are aftereffects to be felt. These can't be rushed. So if a person spends several hours one day reading an entire work in the Bible, and spends the next few days reflecting on it without reading anything else in Scripture, we should be delighted.

This isn't to say that we should *never* read short selections in the Bible and consider them individually. There is a very legitimate place for this activity, so long as these short selections do represent natural literary units. This is how I'll define "studying" the Bible in Chapter 5. But reading must precede studying. This is a specific case of the general principle for approaching any artistic creation: you must engage the whole before you can understand the parts, because their meaning comes from their context within the larger work. And the larger work, by design, is to be appreciated all at once. Thus N.T. Wright insists, "reading the Bible in little snippets . . . is a second-order activity; the primary activity ought to be reading the Bible in large chunks, to get its full flavour and thrust."[7]

I'm not saying that a person shouldn't try to connect with God every day. We need to invest in that relationship. But we can do this in a variety of ways. A "daily quiet time" might just as easily involve journaling or artwork or poetry or song writing, or even a walk in the woods, as a session of Bible reading. A creative response to what a person has experienced in the Scriptures one day can quite properly provide the substance of their devotional activity in the following days. One young woman told me that she was able to do this directly in her copy of *The Books of The Bible* "because there's no distractions, no numbers, no headings, nothing except for the Word." And so, she said, "I draw in it, customize it, write my own song lyrics in it."

So this is the "Bible reading plan" we should teach people to follow: choose a book of the Bible you're interested in; read it; and then, when you're done reading and reflecting, choose another. "'Read' your Bible" (in intense bursts, at intervals), "pray every day, and you'll grow, grow, grow." I suspect that most people would read much more of the Bible, faster, and with more enjoyment and understanding this way than by trying to follow a plan that doled out small portions each day.

But for this new practice to work effectively, a change in the presentation of the Bible is essential. Existing presentations, as we've seen, reinforce the current practice of reading short selections. New presentations like *The Books of The Bible* are needed that will encourage the impulse to read at greater length. Their *form* will implicitly give permission to read the Scriptures continuously, with an eye for meaningful units. Those who've been using this particular new edition report that its format has already been transforming their reading practices.

For one thing, *The Books of The Bible* is encouraging people to "read" the Scriptures in the continuous, enjoyable manner I've said is ideal. One man told me that the format challenged "all my traditional notions about what Bible reading is supposed to look and feel like. Instead of reading a single chapter, I read a story—so much more like all the other reading we do." "I find that I can hardly put the book down once I start reading," another person commented. Another reported on his blog, after his first weekend using the new format, "I've read more of the Bible for sheer pleasure reading in the past 2 days than I've read in the last 2 months." And a professor of New Testament literature, who said he "always wondered what it would be like to actually see the literature through all the debris that tends to collect about the text," said that for him the Bible was now "a real page turner."

Three people who began reading right at the start of *The Books of The Bible* each reported how long it took them to finish the book of Genesis. One said four days; another, three; another, one. When we consider that reading Genesis takes *three weeks* if a person follows a typical read-through-the-Bible plan, we see how readily people will adopt new reading practices, and have a much more fulfilling experience with God's word, as soon as they have resources that give them implicit permission to do so.

Readers also report that they've been able to engage complete compositions more meaningfully. "I loved reading 1 Corinthians in one sitting," a man related. "It's amazing how well the book flows." Another person reported that he'd read Romans "straight through—paragraph by paragraph, thought by thought—just like a book." "There's something immensely freeing about seeing a book as a *book*—a whole unit, like a letter or a piece of poetry or a history—rather than a collection of smaller parts," another noted.

The new presentation is actually steering people away from reading only short selections. One reader told me in an e-mail, "I, and other friends who use *The Books of The Bible*, have definitely found that reading smaller chunks gets harder, as you don't have definitive stopping points and, honestly, you don't want to stop. Rather, you read longer chunks and want to finish the story, the lesson, the letter, or the particular point." Another wrote in his blog, "Instead of coming to a chapter break and unconsciously feeling as though I am 'finished,' I find I am caught up into the story much more, that I want to read further, know more. It's quite refreshing."

But the clearest example I've heard of how the new presentation steers people away from reading only short selections is the story of a young man who tried to use *The Books of The Bible* to read all the way through Scriptures in a single year, in short daily selections. He couldn't divide the edition up by chapters but, seeing that it had about eighteen hundred pages, he figured that if he read five pages a day, he'd finish in about a year. He and a friend set out to read through the Bible this way. But things didn't go the way they expected. "One of the biggest problems," he wrote, "is reading ahead." The description of this as a "problem," even though this was meant humorously, suggests that for some people, traditional Bible reading programs could actually have the unintended consequence of *limiting* how much of the Bible they read. Even if the presentation no longer stops them after short intervals, the accustomed practice might. "I need to read at least this much today" can turn all too easily into "once I've read this much, I've done enough."

And even if it doesn't actually limit us in this way, we can still respond to a Bible reading plan in such a way that reading becomes a duty to be performed, rather than a chance to enjoy a good gift from God. Some of the most encouraging reports I've heard have been from those who've experienced liberation from a felt need to meet an obligation to read a certain amount of the Bible each day. One woman admitted that since she is a "Type A personality," "it *was* all about an every day goal of reading a certain number of chapters." But now, she says, "I am free to just read, instead of trying to accomplish a specific numbered reading task. It is extremely calming and the enjoyment level is definitely heightened." A young man noted similarly, "It's very nice not to have a constant progress check, but just to read every day to a point where the text naturally ebbs." Another man said he was focusing "more on reading than getting my reading done." And a young woman said she was now free to read "without trying to keep track of how much I've read to make sure I've 'read enough,' which helps me to enjoy it more. I read by chunks and stop when I think it makes sense, rather than when I've consumed the allocated number of verses or put in my required time." "Where the Spirit of the Lord is, there is freedom," and, like the readers just quoted, we are meant to experience this same freedom when we take up the word of God.

We may summarize all of these responses, and everything we've been saying about private devotional reading, in the words of one more reader. He recognized perceptively, from his own experience with *The Books of The Bible,* how presentation implies practice and how our current presentations and practices have combined to give us the wrong impression of what the Bible is:

> I would echo the comments of those who have found themselves reading more and larger sections of Scripture at one time. I liken it to the difference between reading a novel and reading

an encyclopedia. An encyclopedia is formatted so that you read a little. A novel captures your attention, stimulates your imagination, and you end up reading more. But here is the thing: you could take the actual text of a novel and format it in an encyclopedia-like fashion and the result would be that you would read less and read it differently. Form and content are tied. That is why I love *The Books of The Bible*. Finally, the Bible is formatted as it should be. When that happens it is read more freely and with a different perspective.

He's right: the Bible isn't an encyclopedia. It's meant to capture our attention and stimulate our imagination. So our practice of "reading" the Bible shouldn't be to take up a prescribed list of short selections each day, out of duty, and then stop. We should dive in and let the flow of the Scriptures carry us away.

Our discussion of "reading" has so far focused on the private, personal, and silent reading characteristic of late modernity. But as we reflect on the practices that could reintroduce the Scriptures in postmodernity, we must acknowledge the "new orality" and post-literacy of that emerging culture. Written text is no longer the primary vehicle (although it remains an important secondary one) through which younger people now obtain information and share experiences with others. Seeing, hearing, and sharing images, words, sounds, voices, and notes has become primary for them. Television, movies, music, and internet audio, video and imagery, accessed through a ever-growing variety of devices, have crowded out books, magazines, and even text-based web pages as the media of choice. So is the community of Jesus' followers working with ever more antiquated technology as it tries to present the Bible—a written text—as God's overture to humanity, no matter what kinds of electronic media it's able to put that written text into?

No—for two important reasons. First, it's not the case that postmodern people can't or don't read, even though they don't *just* read. In order to be post-literate (which our culture is rapidly becoming), you have to be literate in the first place. Young adults are constantly reading and writing (text-messaging, for example). But beyond this, reading, particularly the kind of absorbing and satisfying reading we've been advocating here, remains a powerful vehicle of communication, expression, and enlightenment within the emerging culture. Donald Miller describes the variety of experiences and expressions that now combine to help people reach spiritual insights:

> [T]hey had a certain set of parents and heard a certain song and knew somebody who had a certain experience and saw some movie, read some book, had something happen to them like a car wreck or a trip to Seattle. Then they called on God, and a week later read something in a magazine or met a girl in Wichita, and when all this happened they had an epiphany.[8]

In other words, in postmodernity experience interacts with, and is interpreted by, artistic expressions such as songs, movies, books, and articles. Written materials remain very much part of the mix. And the reactions we're getting from young adults to *The Books of The Bible* show that the Scriptures themselves can remain in the thick of things.

The second reason why the Bible isn't "antiquated technology," even as we move into postmodernity, is that the Bible isn't essentially a written text. Its literary compositions were preserved and transmitted in written form. But all of the Bible was actually composed at a time when writing was, as Walter Ong has put it, essentially a means of recycling into the world of speech words that were originally spoken at some remove in space or time.[9] In other words, the works in the Bible were composed aloud, to be read aloud. (Paul, for instance, would dictate a letter to a scribe, and then send it to a distant church by the hand of a messenger who would read it aloud to a gathering of that community. The prophets, to give another example, would typically speak or even sing their oracles aloud.) Ong notes that the biblical works bear the characteristic marks of oral composition and delivery. "The orality of the mindset in the Biblical text, even in its epistolary sections," he writes, "is overwhelming."[10] This means that none of the biblical works will suffer if they're read aloud and heard aloud, rather than engaged silently on the page. They're actually ideal for the "new orality" of postmodernity.[11]

They will suffer, however, just as much as they do in their written form, if they're read and head aloud only in short selections. Everything we've said about engaging literary compositions in their entirety applies just as much to our hearing them as to our reading them. And so the new practices we'll need for postmodernity will have to include new approaches to the way we read the Bible aloud.

Community worship experiences are one setting in which the Bible has always been read out loud. In premodern times, when the Scriptures (like all books) were rare and expensive, and most people couldn't read, worship was one of the few places where people could find out what was in the Bible. And so the Scripture lessons served two purposes. They were the basis of the liturgy and preaching, and they were also a primary introduction, for many, to the contents of the word of God. In modern times, when most people could read and the typical worshipper owned multiple copies of the entire Bible, Scripture lessons were basically sermon texts. But as we move into postmodernity and biblical literacy has declined steeply, they're once again becoming an important way to introduce people to what the Bible has to say.

But whether in premodern, modern, or postmodern times, the Scriptures have typically been read in worship only in short selections. Practically, there's a limit on how much of the available time can be given to the public reading of Scripture. The rest of the worship experience must be devoted to things like singing, praying, preaching, and sharing the news of the community and its outreach. There are limitations on how long a passage can be discussed meaningfully in a single sermon.

And so the same problems result as with personal, silent reading. In many cases the selections that are read in worship don't correspond with natural units. Pastors who choose their own sermon texts most often select a traditional chapter. Alternatively, they may follow a modern publisher's section divisions. And even if Scripture lessons do correspond with natural units, they're still being encountered in isolation from their wider literary context. Preachers often move around within the Bible from week to week. Even if they preach straight through a book, there may have been no encounter with the book as a whole first. If a church follows the lectionary, the series of short Scripture passages that are read in worship will come from a number of different books. Each passage will take on a secondary level of meaning by association with the words and imagery of the other lectionary passages. This may or may not correspond with the primary meaning it has within the context of its own book. (And because of its authority within the liturgical setting, the lectionary may also subtly influence our understanding of how much Scripture it's appropriate to read at one time.)

Clearly we need to change our practices of public reading just as much as we need to change the approach we've been teaching concerning reading the Scriptures in private devotions. If we want our practices to reflect what the Bible really is, so that modern and postmodern people alike can have a renewed engagement with the word of God, we'll need to read natural units in their entirety when we gather together to worship.

I had the privilege of getting to know Professor John Stek through my work on *The Books of The Bible*. He was the longtime chair of the Committee on Bible Translation, which produced the NIV and TNIV. When he passed away recently, a very meaningful memorial service was held for him at Calvin Seminary, where he'd taught for most of his career. The culmination of the service was a reading of Psalm 103, a personal devotional favorite of his that he'd also published an important study on.[12] His three sons came and stood together at the front of the chapel. One stepped forward and read the opening portion of the psalm, which is a call to praise the LORD "for all his benefits." A second son then read the short assertion of God's reign that follows:

> The LORD works righteousness
> and justice for all the oppressed.

The third son next read the center portion of this psalm, which describes God's character. Then the second son came forward again and read the other brief declaration of God's reign:

> The LORD has established his throne in heaven,
> and his kingdom rules over all.

Finally, the first son read the conclusion, which is another call to praise the LORD. The reading was dramatic and powerful, in the first place, because it was a tribute by sons to their father that celebrated his life's work and his love for the word of God. But it would have had much of the same power in any other setting because of the way separate voices spoke matching parts of the psalm, dramatizing the form and meaning of this eloquent composition.

Contrast this with the unfortunate way many people have only ever encountered Psalm 103 in worship. If they attend churches that use the Revised Common Lectionary, they've actually heard something read from this psalm every year. But they've never heard it in its entirety. And the selections they have heard haven't ever corresponded accurately with any of its natural divisions.[13] It would take only a couple of minutes longer, at most, to read the entire composition.

Giving a higher priority, and thus devoting more time, to reading Scripture aloud in worship would allow people to encounter whole natural units. Multiple readers would be able to illustrate the structure of a work, or bring dialogue to life, or draw out contrasting ideas, in ways that a single reader could not. These are the kinds of new practices we need to develop so that those who join us for our worship experiences can see how meaningful and engaging the Bible really is.

But aren't there practical limits to how much time can be allotted within a worship experience? Psalm 103 is manageable because it's a relatively brief composition. But other "natural units," extending in size all the way up to the longer biblical books, could hardly be read in a single service.

This is true, but we should still try to engage each literary composition in the Bible as a whole before taking up its parts. In the case of group meetings that ordinarily have limited time, a simple expedient can make this possible. A special time can be set aside for the more extended reading that's needed in the case of longer works. This might be a regularly scheduled worship service whose format is adapted. For example, if a book of the Bible were going to be the basis of a series of messages over a number of weeks, it could be read aloud in place of the sermon the first week, with some introductory comments to explain its background and setting. Alternatively, a separate gathering could be held, outside the usual worship time, in which the book would be read out loud. Particularly in cases where a whole church was giving extended and coordinated consideration to a book in all of its worship gatherings, Bible studies, and fellowship groups, this would be an excellent means of "welcoming" the book into the community.

This is very close, in fact, to how the New Testament letters were received by the churches they were originally sent to. They were read aloud in their entirety to gatherings of those communities. The Bible itself records other times when the people of Israel assembled for an extended reading or proclamation of God's word. The book of Deuteronomy, for example, tells us that its contents were originally delivered orally by Moses to a great assembly of the Israelites "in the wilderness east of the Jordan." And after the return from exile, Ezra read "the Book of the Law of Moses" to a special assembly in Jerusalem "aloud from daybreak till noon." So the extended public reading of Scripture is not a postmodern novelty. It's a practice that's part of the heritage of our historic community of faith.

Readers of *The Books of The Bible* have called this to mind as they've seen the literary forms of the biblical writings recaptured in the edition. One pastor told me he could "picture what it would have been like in Colossae when the letter from Paul first arrived and everyone was very excited and gathered around to hear the letter read. How cool would that have been?" Another reader told me that while he could "remember being astonished the first time I learned that the early church read whole epistles at church services," he now thought it would be very appropriate to use the Scriptures in a format like *The Books of The Bible* for "corporate reading at a small group or congregational level." Yet another reader noted, "The Bible is an oral document to be read in community and not just to be studied individually. Paul's letters often were addressed to churches (literally, gatherings) and were read aloud to those congregations. I think this Bible would lend itself to that activity. This is something to which maybe we need to pay more attention." One home study group intentionally modeled their reading on the ancient oral practice when circumstances put many them in the same position as early believers, with no text in hand. They were going to be studying Luke–Acts using *Kingdom Come, Kingdom Go*. Their leader explained to me, "We didn't have enough copies our first night, so some just listened to the reading rather than following along in their other Bibles. We thought that was probably more faithful to the Word's oral tradition and how it was for the first-century saints."

This illustration reminds us that in our day, it's not just whole communities, but also smaller groups within them, that read the Scriptures aloud when they meet. These smaller groups too can begin their study of a book of the Bible by using one meeting to read it (or a significant part of it) aloud together. A campus staff worker who was going to be leading a semester-long study from the first part of Mark recounted what happened when she asked the group to read this whole portion aloud at their first meeting:

I could tell that students were not excited about that when we started, and doubtful of how helpful it would be. But reading it out loud together was engaging. As we read, people could jot notes and thoughts on their manuscripts. We took 30 minutes to read the section, much faster than anyone imagined. Then I gave them time to look for big themes. They did a GREAT job to see big themes and put things together. I was impressed, and they enjoyed it. That set us up well for our semester of studying the book. They knew what was coming in the book and were able to read in depth more in context.

I had a similar experience in a graduate student Bible study I participated in as a volunteer campus staff worker. This group began its consideration of Romans by reading the entire epistle out loud. I brought copies of *The Books of The Bible* for everyone, and we took turns reading sections of the epistle. This took just about an hour, so it fit very well within the usual hour-and-a-half time we devote to reading and discussion. People were surprised that it didn't take any longer. After we finished reading the epistle, the leader asked what our impressions were. Many members spoke about key themes in the epistle: the resurrection life, the relationship of Jew and Gentile, and the relationship of law and Spirit. An international student who was reading the Bible for the first time asked, "What is 'righteousness'?" She very perceptively zeroed in on this term, which is truly a key one in Romans, as essential to understanding everything she'd just heard. And this was in a first-time encounter, in a second language!

The leader himself admitted that in the past he'd always stopped reading Romans "after the first 3 chapters." He would get to the declaration that "all have sinned and fall short of the glory of God, and all are justified freely by his grace through the redemption that came by Christ Jesus," *get himself saved* (as he put it), and not read the rest of the book. Now he saw that this opening part of the epistle flows into an extended discussion of how we can be not just "saved," but transformed by the Spirit. In fact, he noted, all of creation eventually gets in on God's salvation. When he saw how everything in the epistle flowed together, his understanding of salvation was greatly expanded. At the end of the evening one of the participants said, "This was the best Bible study I've ever been in." So a valuable new practice we can adopt in our group Bible studies is to read entire books, or major sections of longer books, aloud together before studying their parts in detail.

In addition to transforming the way the Bible is engaged in contexts where it's traditionally been read out loud, there are some new contexts where also I've heard of the Bible being read aloud, thanks to encouragement *The Books of The Bible* is providing to take innovative approaches. For example, one man reported that he'd started reading the Bible aloud in his private devotions. Recognizing that the Bible, like "all ancient books," was "written to be read aloud," he decided to try this and discovered, "it is so different to read complete sections at a time and to hear the majesty of the words as you read." One staff pastor encouraged the members of his "How to Study the Bible" class to read aloud at home, and the exercise had an impact on the entire congregation. "We encouraged them to read one entire book of the Bible of their choosing," he told me, "but to read it out loud (even if alone) and to read it three times. . . . The result was that they began to ask the church leadership if we could have more Scripture read publicly in our worship services."

I'm sure that creative approaches like these will find their way into even wider settings as our understanding of what it means to "read" the Bible continues to be transformed. I've even heard of two friends getting together to read individual books of the Bible aloud. After reading some shorter books like Jonah ("not the story we both grew up with on the flannel graph in Sunday School," one of them noted), they took up Job and read "the whole thing, in one sitting," changing readers as different characters made their speeches. What's next for these friends? The last I heard, one of them "keeps gunning for Romans," but the other's thinking "we should knock out Genesis instead (or at least first)."

Chapter Five

Studying the Bible after Chapters & Verses:

Understanding the Parts within the Whole

A Bible study group is using a guide called *How to Really Follow Jesus*. This week's lesson is based on a saying of Jesus recorded in the gospel of Matthew: "Anyone who loves their father or mother more than me is not worthy of me; anyone who loves a son or daughter more than me is not worthy of me." The study guide instructs the group to look up a number of other passages in the Bible. It provides chapter and verse numbers so these can be located. The leader gives members different assignments and asks them to read their selections out loud. The first is from Deuteronomy, and it's poetic:

> Your Thummim and Urim belong
> to your faithful servant.

> You tested him at Massah;
> you contended with him at the waters of Meribah.

He said of his father and mother,
"I have no regard for them."

He did not recognize his brothers
or acknowledge his own children,

but he watched over your word
and guarded your covenant.

"What's Thummim?" a member of the group asks. "And who was tested at Massah?" another wants to know. Many seem to share their curiosity. Some in the group remember hearing about Thummim and Massah in other parts of Bible, and they're beginning to recall where. The leader wants to invite them to share what they know, so the group can work these questions out together. But before she can call on them, the person who read the passage glances down to the bottom of the page in her Bible and finds an explanatory note. She reads it out loud. It sounds persuasive, and this ends the discussion.

So the leader calls for the next passage, which is from Zechariah. It concludes, "If some still prophesy, their fathers and mothers, to whom they were born, will say to them, 'You must die, because you have told lies in the LORD's name.' When they prophesy, their own parents will stab them." An awkward silence descends on the room. Everyone shifts uncomfortably in their chairs. The leader quickly asks for the next passage.

This one is from the opening of the book of Ruth, and as it's read, the body language changes. People look a lot more comfortable. They're listening to a story, and it has real human interest.

"Don't urge me to leave you," the young Moabite woman protests to her Israelite mother-in-law. "Your people will be my people and your God my God." When Naomi accepts that Ruth won't be going "back to her people and her gods," the group smiles with the sense of a "happy ending." Ruth has gotten "saved."

After a brief discussion of how Ruth has not "loved father and mother more than God," the group moves on in its study. They don't realize that by leaving the story at this point, they've actually given it a very unhappy ending. Ruth's words to Naomi here are indeed some of the most touching and memorable in the book. They do introduce a key motif. But Ruth isn't safe at all at this point.

Let's leave off the example of this group study to pursue this a bit further. In reality, Naomi has been trying to keep her widowed daughters-in-law from starving to death with her. When she reminds them she has no more sons to give them in marriage, she's stressing that they'll have no male relative to provide for them if they follow her to Israel. Naomi describes the only evident solution: "Go back . . . find rest in the home of another husband." When Ruth defies this counsel, readers are supposed to be filled with suspense, if not dread. They're meant to be drawn forward into the rest of the story to find out whether this young woman paid for her reckless faith with her life.

How will these vulnerable, destitute women be provided for? The rest of the book answers this question. The next scene depicts how Ruth is providentially led to glean in the fields of Naomi's distant but wealthy relative, Boaz, who protects her and provides for her. Later Ruth finds more lasting security as Boaz's wife. Finally she bears a son, Obed, and the women of Bethlehem recognize that he'll become a "family guardian" to Naomi. "Naomi has a son!" they marvel, and they assure her, "He will renew your life and sustain you in your old age." The specter of hunger, the wolf at the door, has driven a single plot through the whole book. At every turn, Ruth and Naomi have been delivered through God's providential care.

And right at the end of the book, the author reveals that Ruth was the great-grandmother of King David. The future destiny of the nation actually depended on these women surviving. Now it becomes evident why the book was written. It's speaking to an audience in the monarchy period, several generations after the events it relates. It appears that some people were disputing whether David could sit on the throne, since he would ordinarily have been excluded from Israelite civic life as the descendant of a Moabite woman. But the way God honored Ruth's daring trust speaks incontestably of her acceptance as one of God's own people. So how could anyone now put the nation's destiny back in jeopardy by trying to disqualify David? Each episode of the book helps bring readers to this conclusion. None conveys its full meaning outside the framework of the book as a whole. The opening scene of the book is not supposed to leave us with a sense of relief or closure. It's designed to set the rest of the plot in motion. It's clear that we will badly misread this scene if we don't understand it in the context of the overall story. At best, it will provide an anecdotal example of faith and courage, but its wider literary, historical, and theological implications will all be lost.

This, unfortunately, is what happens to many of the biblical passages we encounter when we "study." My illustration of the Bible study group was intended to show how our accustomed practices encourage us to take up episodes like this, and their counterparts in other genres (like the poetic stanza from Deuteronomy and the prophecy in Zechariah), as self-contained units. We treat them as if they convey their meaning as independent elements within chains of references running through the Bible (although this meaning may have to be explained further to us by people with specialized knowledge, such as study-guide authors). These practices are derived from the form the Bible was given in modernity and the understanding it encouraged of what the Bible is. But we have to ask ourselves honestly how deeply we've gone into the word of God if our "Bible study" consists of taking up passages without appreciating how they create and receive meaning within their own books.

The example of the study group was fictitious, and intended to be somewhat humorous. Admittedly it didn't represent the "best practice" of even our current methods. Not every contemporary study guide sends people roaming around in the Scriptures this way. My example was based, however, on the cross references one resource provided for the saying of Jesus the group in the example was trying to understand. And so any real group that relied on this same resource could have an experience much like the one described.

Indeed, such an experience may actually be much closer to fact than fiction. One person who got a copy of *The Books of The Bible* wrote on a blog that he "loved it" for reading, but he questioned whether an edition without chapters and verses would be "practical" for activities such as "group study," since participants wouldn't be able to refer the group to other passages in the Bible efficiently. Another person wrote in response:

> Perhaps my experience is different from others, but how many people in a Bible study "spontaneously" think of other other Bible passages to refer to? More commonly, such jumping around seems to occur in the following situations:
>
> a) A group is studying First Corinthians. Someone pipes in saying, "My Bible has a note that refers to Mark 85:15 which says . . ." Everyone flips to that verse, reads it, and is then baffled as to how that clarifies the original passage in question, thus bringing discussion to a halt.
>
> b) The study guide that the group is using, instead of focusing on the book in question, has people jumping all over looking at other randomly selected verses. Suspicious types conclude that the whole exercise is a way for the author of the study guide to push his or her own agenda. Others conclude that making sense of the Bible is impossible without such helps that tell you which random passages should be strung together

(since the order they are actually in is apparently not helpful).

This person declared that if *The Books of The Bible* made this kind of approach to "studying" more difficult, or even impossible, that would actually be a good thing.

This comment is very pertinent to our discussion, for several reasons. First, it confirms that people actually do experience some of the things I've described in their Bible studies: participants citing notes that shut down discussion and guides that send them to scattered passages instead of "focusing on the book in question." But this comment also reflects a postmodern suspicion of authority. And it clearly recognizes the message sent by the modern form of the Bible and the practices we've developed around it: "making sense of the Bible is impossible without such helps that tell you which random passages should be strung together (since the order they are actually in is apparently not helpful)."

I expect that it will become increasingly more difficult to conduct "studies" this way as we move farther into postmodernity. People who'll want to see and experience things for themselves, in the flow and complexity of their natural settings, will resist approaches that refer them to passages in isolation from their contexts. They won't be content to just look up the "right answers." There will be an even greater suspicion of the agendas of those in authority. People who are starting out disaffected from the Bible won't want to explore it if they're given the impression it's a bunch of statements put together in the wrong order that are "impossible to make sense of" unless someone else tells you how. If Bible study is to be meaningful and successful in postmodernity, I believe we'll need a significantly different understanding of what "studying" is.

I was recently part of an actual group that was looking at the book of Daniel. When we took up the third episode in the book, the participants were fascinated to hear how Nebuchadnezzar made a statue ninety feet high out of gold. Some of them glanced down at the notes in their Bibles and read them out loud to try to help the group understand this story better. One note suggested that this was an ostentatious display of the wealth, power, and prosperity of the empire. Another observed that a huge gold statue would have been overwhelmingly bright and dazzling. But I asked the members of the study to consider whether anything we'd encountered earlier in the book of Daniel would explain why Nebuchadnezzar made this statue out of gold.

They thought back to the previous episode, which we'd discussed the week before, and remembered that the king had had a dream about a statue. Its head was made of gold, but its chest and arms were silver, its torso and thighs were bronze, its legs were iron, and its feet were made of iron and clay. Daniel's interpretation of the dream was that Nebuchadnezzar's empire, symbolized by the gold head, would be displaced by an inferior empire, which would then be replaced by another, and another, in the years to come. In light of this dream and its interpretation, our group recognized that Nebuchadnezzar created a statue that was entirely gold to offer a direct and very public rejection of the message he'd received from God. He was saying, using the very symbolism of the dream God sent him, that his own empire would actually last forever and never be displaced. And by insisting that all the officials in his kingdom bow down to this statue, he was requiring them to join him in contradicting God's revealed vision of the future, and to give their allegiance to him and his empire instead. No wonder Daniel's friends felt they had to disobey!

This is studying. Our group wouldn't have found satisfying answers to its questions, and we'd have missed an essential dynamic within the book, if we'd simply "read the notes" and moved on. We got a much greater insight into the passage when we understood how it functioned within the book of Daniel.

But we haven't been trained to study this way in modernity. We haven't been taught that we need to *read* first in order to be able to *study* afterward. In fact, we haven't been encouraged to "read" at all, not in the continuous way I described in Chapter 4. We've just been presented with isolated parts of larger works, without being shown how they fit within a whole book and how we can appreciate the meaning they have there. We've been encouraged to try to understand them instead by looking to other isolated biblical passages in series of cross-references, or by consulting the notes in our Bibles, study guides, and commentaries, and by asking our pastors, teachers, and group leaders.

In other words, this has been our definition of studying: *moving back and forth between the text and explanatory resources*. This approach to Bible "study" isn't effective. The units it engages often aren't the structurally and thematically meaningful ones within a book. Even when they are, we don't appreciate the meaning they receive from their place within the book as a whole. This kind of studying can easily devolve into a running commentary on interesting or puzzling features of an ill-defined stretch of text. It depends on people having an implicit trust in the knowledge and trustworthiness of group leaders and the authors of notes and guides.

We'll need to adopt a new definition of studying: *considering the parts of a biblical book closely and carefully to understand their place within the book as a whole.* This means that studying has to be the second step in a process whose first step is reading. Yes, in a third step, we should eventually seek to situate the individual parts of a composition within their wider biblical context, that is, in relation to thematically similar passages elsewhere in the Scriptures. "Cross-references," in this sense, can shed light on a passage. But we must turn to them only after we've understood it in its immediate context. To paraphrase Tip O'Neill's famous maxim about politics, in the Bible, "All meaning is local," initially. (Even when passages can only be understood in light of quotations or allusions they make to other Scriptures, like the passage cited above from Deuteronomy, their *meaning* still consists in the message they convey in relationship to the material that immediately surrounds them. This passage is designed to describe the distinct position of Levi within the tribes of Israel, not primarily to call individuals away from family ties to a higher loyalty.)

And when we use external interpretive materials, this must be to help answer questions that come from our own interaction with a passage. We shouldn't let these materials supply the questions for us. We should be careful to turn to them only when our personal and group resources of reflection and discussion have been exhausted. "Commentaries," one of my seminary professors used to warn, "are thought stoppers." He meant that the habit of turning immediately to commentaries (or similar resources, such as study notes) shuts down our own personal process of reflection and discovery. External resources can be used very valuably as a final supplement to this process. But if they're used as a substitute for it, they indeed become "thought stoppers." (One reader of *The Books of The Bible*, aware of this dynamic, wrote to ask us not to create a "study Bible" version of the edition. The ease of relying on notes, he insisted, would "kill Bible study and discovery," which he said the format was making possible for him in new ways.)

This new understanding of what it means to "study" the Bible can be described by analogy to the way we interact with other art forms. What's the difference, for example, between watching a film and studying a film? When you watch, you sit back and enjoy the whole thing, suspending your critical faculties and entering into an aesthetic experience. When you later study this film, you think analytically about what you've seen. You identify key thematic and transitional scenes and watch them again individually, perhaps repeatedly, to appreciate how they work and how they contribute to the film as a whole. You might listen to the director's commentary, if it's available. But would anyone attempt to "study" a film before watching it all the way through first? Would they feel they had "watched" it at all if they'd only seen selected individual scenes, perhaps compared with similar scenes from other movies? Would anyone watch a film for the first time while listening to the director's commentary, shifting their attention back and forth between the action that was unfolding and what was being said about it, in the belief that this was how they were meant to understand it? Certainly not. So why should we "study" the books in the Bible, which are all creative compositions like a film, in isolated pieces?

Unfortunately, the way the text of Scripture is presented in our Bibles may be sending a strong visual message that we should consider it in pieces. In many Bibles, the text is dwarfed by notes and features that nearly crowd it off the page. The words of Scripture don't appear, to use another art form as an illustration, like a painting hung on the wall of a gallery, to be experienced as a whole and then appreciated for its individual parts. Instead, we encounter them like a papyrus fragment displayed in a glass museum case that's surrounded by extensive interpretive material because there's no other way to make sense of it. It's time to change the picture of studying in our minds, and the corresponding visual imagery that our Bibles present, so that as intriguing questions arise in our consideration of specific passages, we will be drawn not to the notes on the bottom of the page, or to references elsewhere in the Scriptures, but into the surrounding text of the larger composition to answer them.

In other words, our *presentations* of the Bible need to showcase books-as-a-whole and highlight the text, not the notes or cross-references. That way our Bibles will send a visual message about what reading really is and about what studying really is. We can then develop study *practices* around these presentations that will equip people to find the meaning of individual passages first by understanding their place in the book they're part of, not by turning to external resources or looking up other passages in Scripture.

Readers of *The Books of The Bible* are reporting that the new edition is encouraging precisely this approach to studying. One of them wrote that the new format was helping him "get a greater grasp of the movement of the works and the purpose of each section." Another reported that he was doing his "real study out of it. I am trying to reason my way to passages now and get a better idea of the content of each book." Several readers noted that they were now relying much less on external resources and cross-references. One of them wrote,

> I have been studying the Bible without outside influence, thanks to *The Books of The Bible*. I don't use a commentary, I don't go through the lexicon or Strong's numbers and parse verbs. I sit with the Scriptures. I read them over. I meditate on them. I stretch them out in my mind and reflect on them.

Another noted that the new edition

> allows the Bible to be read and studied the way other books are read and studied. A lot of the traditional approaches—isolating phrases out of context and linking them to similar phrases elsewhere, exhaustive "word studies" that put an enormous

weight on word choice at the expense of thought/ argument structures—not only don't work in such a [format] but would never arise naturally from it. Instead of creating pedants and antiquarians, the format facilitates the formation of literate Bible readers.

One reader even predicted that as Bibles whose format highlighted natural literary structures became more widely available, "most of the more academic-in-nature tools (commentaries, dictionaries, chapter-and-verse Bibles) might very well find themselves drawn upon less and less." They will at least be drawn upon, we may hope, more appropriately, and be allowed to foster natural curiosity rather than suppress it.

One of the main goals of *The Books of The Bible* is to free individuals and groups to do precisely this kind of independent, inductive exploration. However, it's not appropriate to leave people entirely on their own. The knowledge, insights, and interpretations that have been stored up over the centuries within the community of God's people, and which continue to be granted to teachers and scholars today, are an indispensable resource for understanding the Bible. The Scriptures are meant to be engaged in community, not in isolation. That is why we worked carefully, as we were developing the format for *The Books of The Bible*, to strike a proper balance between encouraging individual investigation and situating it within its appropriate community context. On the one hand, as we explain in the

Preface to the edition, "Footnotes, section headings and other supplemental materials have been removed from the page in order to give readers a more direct and immediate experience of the word of God." But on the other hand, we included introductions to the books of the Bible and its major divisions "to provide background information." Beyond this, as I noted in Chapter 3, we encouraged readers to "study the Bible in community."[1]

And since the resources of tradition include not just the insights of those we encounter personally, but the entire legacy of scholars and teachers from other places and times, it's desirable and advantageous for relevant insights from their work to be made available to us, to inform our own reading and study. Once we have placed these scholarly resources in their appropriate supporting role, in fact, we can more properly interpret the visual signals that resources like our current "study Bibles" send. Their notes and features are not actually threatening to displace the text; rather, they represent the wider community surrounding readers and informing their own process of discovery. But presentations like this may still encourage a tendency to rely on notes as a substitute for active investigation. This tendency must always be resisted, so it's best to understand and use study Bibles as specialized tools, rather than as general-purpose Bibles. The inappropriate use of a study Bible will always trump a group leader's most careful preparations and its members' most inquisitive explorations.

As individuals and groups begin to engage the Bible by reading whole books and then studying their natural parts, another expression of "tradition" or community resourcing—the study guide—will take on a new, more vital role. Many of the biblical writings are composed in unfamiliar ancient genres, which may be difficult for contemporary readers to appreciate without some initial assistance. The appropriate parts to consider within these writings may also not be readily evident. This will be particularly true if readers are accustomed to engaging these works through chapter and section divisions that don't accurately reflect their natural structures. And so there's a mandate for a new generation of Bible study guides to be created. Some current guides largely trace chains of references through the Scriptures. Others examine a single book, but still go through it chapter by chapter. These new guides will aim specifically to equip people first to make an informed reading of a biblical book as a whole, and then to study its natural parts with a view toward recognizing how they create and receive meaning within the whole. This will provide a deeper understanding of the Scriptures that will inform believers' attitudes, decisions, and perspectives over the long term. I will be working with Biblica Publishing in the years ahead to help develop a series of such guides. So far, *John* and *Genesis* have been published in their UNDERSTANDING THE BOOKS OF THE BIBLE series. I hope that many other scholars, writers, and publishers will work to create similar resources.

But won't there still be a place for guides that don't move section by section through books, but rather pursue a topic of interest throughout the Bible, to help people understand the full counsel of God on that subject? I would agree that guides like these will remain valuable. But they will have to be constructed more carefully in the future, because the "agendas" behind them will be regarded with such suspicion. Any impression they create that the materials in the Bible are jumbled and need to be rearranged will only deepen disaffection with the Scriptures themselves. Such guides will likely need to consider fewer passages over the same number of lessons, in greater detail, and with more attention to their place within whole books.

In fact, studying just one longer book might allow a group to investigate a topic that's of major interest in that book. For example, the group I described at the beginning of this chapter might have used some key sayings of Jesus found in the gospel of Matthew to examine what that book as a whole has to say about "how to really follow Jesus." Once they'd become familiar with the entire work and its overall structure, they could use a given saying each week to get into it further. When they took up the saying about "not loving father and mother more than Jesus," the leader could ask various members to examine different natural parts of the book to identify where this saying was illus-trated in Jesus' life and in the lives of his followers. Studies like this would help correct the approach to the gospels (and the rest of the Bible) that developed in the course of modernity, an approach that one person described this way, by contrast with the presentation in *The Books of The Bible*:

> We think of the four Gospels as repositories of fragmentized selections of Jesus' ministry. Rather than approaching Matthew, for example, as a his-torical literary narrative on the teachings and life of

Jesus with consistent flow, character, and internal harmony, we approach it almost as if it were a chronologically-arranged newspaper in which each event is not readily expected to correlate with the next. Regrettably, we have learned to comprehend the Bible as a compendium of individual verses or passages.

In this chapter I've been insisting that "studying" the Bible should not be envisioned as moving back and forth between the biblical text and external resources. Rather, we should understand studying as the task of situating individual passages within their primary context of meaning: the book they form a part of. However, we've also seen that external resources in general, properly handled, do have a vital role to play in support of this enterprise. And in particular, they will have a specialized role in the years ahead. They will inform and guide us as we move from the fragmented, cross-referenced Bible of modernity to a new conception of the Scriptures as a collection of literary creations that should first be read in their entirety and then studied in their natural parts.

But if people want to move from "reading" to "studying," as I've defined those activities, how can they identify the meaningful smaller units they should be seeking to understand within a larger work? In other words, if studying consists in giving focused consideration to these units, how are readers to recognize them in the first place?

Ideally, over time, through new presentations and practices, the habit of relying on chapters and verses will be broken, and a new skill will be built into the repertoire of pastors, teachers, and students: recognizing the signals that the biblical authors themselves are sending about the structures of their works. But on the way there, it will be useful for some kind of resource beyond the text to help point the way. Such a resource has actually been embedded within the format of *The Books of The Bible:* the line spacing of varying width that indicates larger and smaller units within the biblical compositions.

Here's one example of how this line spacing works. There's an extended oracle in the book of Isaiah that rebukes the people of Judah and Jerusalem for not trusting in their God and for seeking foreign alliances to protect them from the encroaching Assyrian empire. It begins by using Samaria, the decadent capital of the neighboring kingdom of Israel, as an object lesson, and it concludes by passing judgment on Assyria itself. But throughout the oracle, the people of Judah are the main target.

This oracle marks off its individual parts by pronouncing specific "woes." It's common for prophetic oracles to be structured by a repeated phrase in this way. The first five parts begin:

"Woe to that wreath, the pride of Ephraim's drunkards"

"Woe to you, Ariel, Ariel, the city where David settled!"

"Woe to those who . . . hide their plans from the Lord"

"Woe to the obstinate children"

"Woe to those who go down to Egypt for help"

The last part is marked with a double woe:

> "Woe to you, destroyer, you who have not been destroyed!

> Woe to you, betrayer, you who have not been betrayed!"

Thus, while the oracle as a whole has six parts, it proclaims seven woes, a number symbolic of completeness. When we let the oracle's own structural signals guide us through it, we see how its form and content work together to express the prophet's message.

Ideally our presentations of the Bible will make this natural form apparent. In *The Books of The Bible*, the entire oracle is set off from the rest of the book of Isaiah by four lines of white space at its beginning and end. Within the oracle, each of the parts introduced by woes is separated by two lines of white space. The smaller units of poetry and prose within these parts are marked off by one line. While the spacing in *The Books of The Bible* suggests these structural divisions, it doesn't send a signal to stop reading; the eye flows easily across the spaces into the following material. Rather, the spacing guides the reader visually through a continuous reading of the extended oracle, paced by suitable pauses along the way. And when readers return to study this oracle within the book of Isaiah, six natural parts to consider in more detail are readily apparent.

Contrast this with how our customary presentations take us through the Bible. If we rely on the traditional chapter divisions, we really have no way of knowing that we should treat this oracle as a distinct unit within the book. The chapter numbers run in a steady sequence right through Isaiah, making any larger units indistinguishable from the surrounding material. Reading plans could potentially help here, but plans like the ones I described in Chapter 4 don't respect the boundaries of this oracle. They don't assign it to be read as a distinct unit on a single day, or even over the course of two or three days. Instead, readers encounter its opening part on one day, grouped with some material that precedes; they're then assigned the middle part on one or more subsequent days; and finally they read the closing part with material that follows in the book of Isaiah.

But if we were using chapters as our guide, and we did somehow know that all of the material in this oracle belonged together, we would at least see it as a composition with six parts, since it represents chapters 28–33 in the traditional scheme. But we'd still have the wrong six parts: the second and third woes are combined in chapter 29, while the fifth woe is divided into chapters 31 and 32. We'd have a distorted idea of the oracle's form and of how that form structures its content. This is why Bible presentations need to be created that will dispense with chapters and verses and instead show what the larger and smaller natural units in the biblical books are.

Creating such presentations calls for both humility and charity. As I acknowledged in Chapter 3, various interpreters who are equally well informed and who are equally careful scholars of the Scriptures may reach differing conclusions about a biblical book's structure. I'm not insisting that the understandings reflected in *The Books of The Bible* are somehow better or more correct than other interpretations. But I do want to argue that the respect we should properly have for the work of other scholars shouldn't prevent us from embedding a reasonable understanding of natural literary structure directly, although subtly, into the text of published editions of the Scriptures. This is needed to help readers develop the new skill of recognizing appropriate individual parts to "study" once they've read a book as a whole.

Many contemporary versions of the Bible include section divisions that represent the translators' understanding of at least the smaller parts of books. At the same time, however, the publishers leave chapter and verse divisions in place, and this provides an effective disclaimer that they're not trying to move readers to a new interpretive grid. I would argue, however, that we should try to move readers to a new grid through the form of our published editions. "Studying," the consideration of parts within the whole, is going to happen, one way or another. It's a necessary and appropriate activity as we engage the Bible. The only question is, how will people identify the parts they should be studying? If we don't try to point readers to books' natural structures, by default they will continue to use chapters and verses, or else they will rely on section divisions (contrary to publishers' intentions) to guide them.

This is why, in developing *The Books of The Bible*, we not only removed chapters, verses, and section headings, but also added what is admittedly an extratextual resource, the line spacing. This spacing is designed to be self-effacing; it's intended only to facilitate readers' own engagement with literary compositions. We don't claim to have definitively identified the structures of all the biblical books. We look forward to interacting with, and learning from, other scholars as the project of suggesting natural structure through the format of Scripture moves forward. As I explained in Chapter 3, we've only tried to represent the biblical authors' own indications of literary structure. As one reader, grasping this approach, explained on his blog:

> Although there are no headings, the designers have attempted to show how the writers indicated divisions in their books, by the judicious use of paragraphing, indentation and spacing. It is suggested that [literary structure] was originally shown [in the biblical writings] by repetition of a phrase, change of topic, movement in place or time and by changing from one kind of writing to another. This is one of the most helpful aspects of the new Bible.

Naturally some interpreters may disagree that is the proper method to follow in seeking to identify literary structures. Others may question whether we have employed this method successfully in all cases. But *The Books of The Bible* does represent an attempt to displace the chapter-and-verse grid with a more natural account of literary structure, and as such, it represents a resource that should promote better reading and studying of the Bible.

Readers of the edition have been very appreciative of this resource. It seems to be guiding them as they make their own determinations of literary structure. One young man reported, "The guys in my house have all been doing a study on 1 Peter, and when we went hunting for divisions and structure, the decisions you all made in there were so key to helping us chunk it up." A campus staff worker told me, "For my Bible study preparations, I have to decide how much Scripture to try to teach each week. I use *The Books of The Bible* to figure out where to break sections. This sometimes goes against what I've first been taught, but as I step back and look at the bigger picture, I often find myself falling in line with *The Books of The Bible*." One pastor told me that when he used the edition, he felt "better able to navigate and recognize the *organic* divisions in the text." Another pastor reported that he had "utilized the structure" implicitly indicated in *The Books of The Bible* to choose his Scripture lessons for a series of messages from the gospel of Matthew. And another young man reported,

> I have become a more active reader: while I read, I realize that while the chapter and verse numbers are "artificial" additions of an editor, so are the formatting choices made by the editors of *The Books of The Bible*. This isn't to say that I necessarily disagree with any of the formatting choices (I don't . . . yet), but just that I think more actively about how form affects meaning.

If, as I've argued throughout this chapter, studying needs to be re-defined as the quest to understand how the parts of a book function within the whole, then the first step in studying is to recognize what those parts are. It's encouraging to see how the formatting of *The Books of The Bible* has led readers to think more carefully and deliberately about how they should "chunk up" the biblical writings, without making them feel this decision has already been made for them.

Chapter Six

Preaching the Bible after Chapters & Verses:

Situating a Story within a Story

O ne Sunday morning, after sharing the latest
news in the life of our church, I stepped out of
the pulpit and walked down the chancel steps to
stand at the head of our sanctuary's center aisle. I invited
all the children who were with us in worship that morning
to come forward. I explained that I had a special message
for them before they left for their classes. I sat down on
the steps, and when they'd been seated all around me, I
pulled on a pair of thermal mitts. I then picked up a long-
handled spatula in one hand and a set of tongs in the other.

"What am I getting ready to do?" I asked the children.

"Grill?" one of them ventured, after a short pause.

"Exactly," I replied.

Another child spoke up. "My dad grills all the time,
even in the winter."

"I don't see why he shouldn't," I responded. "It's really
never too cold to grill."

After a little more banter I said, "Let me tell you how I got a grill of my own." I shared how my wife and I had been out for a walk in our neighborhood one day when we came upon an older-looking grill that had been set out by the curb. The garbage wasn't going to be collected until later in the week, so we wondered whether someone hadn't gotten a new grill and put this old one out for anyone who wanted it. We lifted the lid and began to verify that all the parts were there and in working order. As we were doing this, a man walked up. He had a dog on a leash. ("It was one of those big white dogs with black spots," I specified. "Do any of you know what they're called?" "*Dalmatians*," several children shouted together.)

I told them how my wife and I took up defensive positions around the grill. We'd seen it first, and this man couldn't just walk up and claim it. Why did he insist on standing there, trying to talk to us? But then the lights came on for both of us at exactly the same moment. This was the man who'd put the grill out by the curb! He'd been out walking his dog and was just getting back to his house. Immediately we started treating him entirely differently. We became warm and conversational, answering his questions about whether we had a grill (we didn't) and what we thought of this one (we liked it). We looked at him expectantly and appreciatively. "Well, if you're interested," he offered, "I also have the manual and a wire brush I could give you to clean it." Yes, we said, we'd be very interested. He agreed to move the grill away from the curb so no one else would take it while we went to get our car so we could pick it up. We thanked him repeatedly as we left, and also when we returned to make the pickup.

And that, I told the children, was how we got our grill. But, I asked, what had made us suddenly treat the man so differently? "At first you thought he was going to take something from you," one perceptive child observed, "but when you realized he wanted to give you something, you started being nice to him instead." "That's just what happened," I agreed, over laughter from the congregation. I then explained to the children that it's the same way in our relationship with God: when we start treating God with real appreciation, that's a sign that we've realized all the wonderful things God wants to give us.

The children went off to their classes, and I then preached a sermon to the "grownups" from the book of Colossians. As a pastor, I always coordinated my children's messages with the ones the adults would hear, so that families could talk together about the theme of the morning. In my sermon I explained the role that thankfulness plays in this epistle, and in Paul's wider theology, as a marker of grace accepted and acknowledged. "Just as you received Christ Jesus as Lord, continue to live your lives in him . . . overflowing with thankfulness," Paul writes at one key point in Colossians. "Be thankful," he admonishes later; have "gratitude in your hearts." This is normative for the Christian life. Situating this epistle within Paul's wider writings, I noted that he used thanksgiving even more directly in Romans as a marker of grace: "although they knew God, they neither glorified him as God nor gave thanks to him." At the end of the sermon, I challenged the people to consider whether they recognized themselves as recipients of grace from the thankfulness to God they felt in their hearts.

After this service several adults told me that they'd understood the sermon much better because of the children's message. This was not unusual. Some weeks, in fact, people went so far as to say that they *wouldn't* have understood the sermon if it hadn't been for the children's message. The church was near a college campus and it attracted many students. One student's parents attended worship a couple of times at the start of his freshman year and a few more times afterward. He later told me that when they called him on Sunday afternoons to see how he was doing, their first question usually was, "What did the pastor say this morning *in his children's message*?" When I performed the wedding of a student who'd attended this church, some years after her graduation, she asked me to include a children's message in her marriage service. (I was glad to. I brought a tarnished silver tray and slowly polished it for the children as I explained that there's a "beauty within" that a loving husband or wife can see and draw forth from their spouse. My sermon text was from the Song of Songs, where the lovers describe the beauty they see in one another.)

Why were adults, even the oldest ones in the church, so interested in these messages, which were supposed to be for the children? Why, for many people, did they actually provide the key to understanding the sermon? I'm convinced it was because the sermons represented a form that was becoming increasingly inaccessible to people, while the children's messages were in a form that was becoming more and more accessible, or that perhaps had always been accessible.

The sermons I was preaching were in a modern form. They operated on modern assumptions about what truth is and how people grasp it. They rested ultimately on logical arguments that appealed to the rational faculties. The children's messages, by contrast, were stories, related in an informal conversational setting, illustrated with visual aids and containing other visual elements within them (e.g., the Dalmatian). They were interactive and sensory, and they appealed to common experience.

All of these things made them better suited than the sermons to communicate to the culture that was taking shape around us. While the congregation included people from both sides of the modern-postmodern divide (senior citizens as well as college students), they were already living together in a culture where electronic media had become the information source of choice and appeal to personal experience had replaced reasoned, sequential argument as the primary means of persuasion. The children's messages, as a visual and anecdotal medium, were actually needed to provide a means of access back into the rational framework of the sermon for people in a culture that had largely moved past its way of organizing and communicating information.

The children's messages would actually have been accessible to people in most times or places. They weren't so much postmodern as non-modern. We don't expect younger children to be capable of following a rational argument, and so we try to communicate spiritual truths to them through stories and pictures. The use of this method reflects an implicit assumption that people have a primal ability to respond to these things from an early age. Reasoning emerges later and eventually becomes a vital part of a person's capacity to understand life, develop a coherent belief system, and communicate meaningfully with others. But modernity, as we see it more and more in retrospect, was an overvaluing of the rational, analytical faculty, an overestimation of its capacity to enable us to make sense of our world, and a consequent undervaluing of sensory, experiential, aesthetic ways of knowing. Modernity moved children too fast from "What a pretty picture!" to "That makes sense." The advent of postmodernity is giving us the opportunity to rebalance the appeals we make to various faculties. If we are careful not to undervalue any of them, we will be able to communicate the message of the Scriptures meaningfully to coming generations.

My particular interest in this chapter will be to ask how this message can be communicated through preaching from the Bible in its natural form. What new practices will this call for and make possible? To answer this question, let's begin by considering our present practice.

The modern sermon takes many forms, but in essence its goal is always the same. It may trace a chain of cross-references through the Bible, with listeners flipping pages as the preacher calls out the numbers. Conversely, it may consider a topic of interest in light of one particular selection from the Scriptures. Or a sermon may be part of

Figure 1.

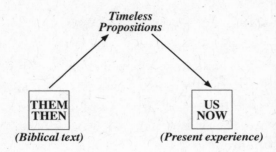

an expository series that moves sequentially through an entire book. But in each case, the task of the sermon is to derive something from the text—doctrines, principles, or instructions—that we can then apply to ourselves. The operating assumption is that the connection between "us now" and the biblical witness to the faith and experience of "them then"[1] is made via timeless propositions that lie behind the text of Scripture[2] and that can be extracted from it for our own guidance. (See Figure 1.) As we've noted, the shape the Bible has been given in modernity reflects and reinforces this assumption. The Scriptures are presented physically and visually as a series of numbered and sequenced statements, evocative of timeless propositions (even though these statements still have to be pulled apart and rearranged for a coherent system to emerge.)

Non-modern preaching understands its purpose differently. Its basic task is to situate a story within a story. This is what my children's message about the grill did. It showed how one episode in my personal life formed part of the larger story of God's gracious dealings with humanity. Gordon Fee, when summarizing the overall message of Paul's writings, says that for Paul, "salvation is grace, and ethics is gratitude."[3] In my story, I embraced an "ethic of gratitude" as soon as I recognized myself as the recipient of grace from another human being. Once this picture had been created, the analogy between God and the man with the dog wasn't hard to draw, to show how my story fit into the larger one.

This approach to preaching and teaching is modeled for us continually in the Scriptures. They arose in a non-modern context and so continually use the universal means of stories and pictures to communicate spiritual truths. As this collection of inspired writings takes shape, the biblical authors draw on more and more stories and pictures from the earlier Scriptures (that is, the ones that had been created and transmitted by their own day) in order to situate their audience within the greater biblical story. Pierre Grelot calls these "figurative symbols." He explains that they depend on "the close relationship, which is exclusively biblical, between the revelation that has been put into writing in the scriptural texts and the historical experience of the community within which these texts were written."[4]

Consider, for example, Stephen's sermon in Acts, when he defends himself before the Sanhedrin. He doesn't try to refute the charges against him logically and sequentially. Instead, he *retells the story of Israel*, from Abraham, Isaac, and Jacob through Moses to David, in order to situate his hearers within that story. By identifying which characters his accusers correspond to, he shows them how they, by their actions, have actually been continuing the story. "You are just like your ancestors," he insists. "You always resist the Holy Spirit! Was there ever a prophet your ancestors did not persecute? They even killed those who predicted the coming of the Righteous One. And now you have betrayed and murdered him." Ironically, in response to the sermon, the Sanhedrin members carry their part of story even further. They stone Stephen to death in a rage, killing one more herald of the Righteous One. But Stephen adds his own personal episode to the story of Jesus, who said on the cross, "Father, forgive them." As he is dying himself, Stephen prays, "Lord, do not hold this sin against them."

Paul, as he defends his own ministry in a number of speeches recorded in Acts, takes the same approach of situating one story within another. To answer the questions that Jewish and Roman officials have about what in the world he is doing (or what he is doing to the world), he tells his own story. But he implicitly situates it within the story of God's people. His defense before King Agrippa is typical. He relates his strict upbringing within Judaism, his initial hostility to the followers of Christ, and the encounter with the risen Jesus on the road to Damascus that made him a fervent apostle of the very faith he once tried to destroy. But Paul describes the specific charge he received from Jesus in these words: "I am sending you to [the Gentiles] to open their eyes and turn them from darkness to light." At the conclusion of his speech, he uses similar words as he more directly situates his story within a larger one: "I am saying nothing beyond what the prophets and Moses said would happen—that the Messiah would suffer and, as the first to rise from the dead, would bring the message of light to his own people and to the Gentiles."

In both cases, the image of a "light for the Gentiles" is an allusion to Isaiah. God said through that prophet that his "servant" would be a "light for the Gentiles, that my salvation may reach to the ends of the earth." The "servant" in Isaiah is an evocative figure, sometimes representing the people of Israel, sometimes the prophet himself, sometimes contemporary figures God is working through such as King Cyrus, and sometimes a later individual who will be a definitive agent of salvation. By describing his own apostolic mandate in the words of the biblical servant's job description, Paul is saying implicitly that his own life and ministry are the latest chapter in the big story of the "servant of Yahweh," a story that Isaiah had already traced through redemptive history as he knew it into the current events of his own day and forward into the future. (In his second sermon in Pisidian Antioch, recorded earlier in Acts, Paul makes the connection between his calling and the servant's vocation even more explicit, through a direct quotation from Isaiah: "This is what the Lord has commanded us: 'I have made you a light for the Gentiles, that you may bring salvation to the ends of the earth.'")

But the clearest example of Scriptural modeling of preaching and teaching through biblical stories and images is no doubt found in the parables of Jesus. We already recognize these as striking and challenging stories that evoke a spiritual response, as listeners must make a "forced choice" to identify with one or another of their characters or situations. ("Which of these three do you think was a neighbor to the man who fell into the hands of robbers?" Jesus asked, for example, after telling the parable of the Good Samaritan. When the expert in the law replied, "The one who had mercy on him," Jesus challenged him to identify with this character in his own actions: "Go and do likewise.") We should also appreciate, however, that Jesus' parables often situate themselves, through their symbolic imagery, within the larger story of God, and thus place their listeners, whom they've drawn into their own story-world, within that larger story as well.

For example, one of Jesus' parables is about a man who plants a vineyard. As recorded in Matthew, it describes how the man puts a fence around it, digs a winepress, builds a watchtower, and then leases this vineyard out to tenants. But they don't give him his share of the fruit. They mistreat the servants he sends to collect it, and they ultimately kill his son when he comes as his father's personal emissary. Listeners, as the story speaks to their own relationship with God, may recognize that they are like the tenants who are denying the owner his due. They may even identify with the messengers who are suffering as the master's representatives. But while the story is intended to evoke this kind of response, it pursues further designs as well, and it does this by allusion to an earlier telling of the story of God. (Indeed, if this parable were not situated somehow within this larger story, serious misunderstandings could result. For example, sharecroppers who were being exploited by oppressive landlords would hear the parable and naturally side with the tenants, applauding their resistance, if it weren't made clear that the landlord in this case is supposed to represent a fair and benevolent God.)

The opening details of the parable make a direct allusion to one of Isaiah's oracles, his "song of the vineyard." It similarly describes a vineyard being planted with a surrounding hedge, a watchtower, and a winepress. This vineyard too does not yield the fruit its owner expected: instead of cultivated grapes, it produces only wild ones, as it would have if the vines had never been tended and pruned. Isaiah says this vineyard will therefore be abandoned and the land returned to a fallow state. He then interprets the symbolism of this oracle:

> The vineyard of the LORD Almighty
> is the house of Israel,
>
> and the people of Judah
> are the vines he delighted in.
>
> And he looked for justice, but saw bloodshed;
> for righteousness, but heard cries of distress.

The abandonment of the vineyard represents the impending end of the nation in conquest and exile, as punishment for the injustice and oppression it has practiced. This will happen even though the nation believes itself to be secure as the chosen people of God.

Jesus tells his own listeners that they will similarly forfeit the position of spiritual privilege they take for granted: "the kingdom of God will be taken away from you and given to a people who will produce its fruit." He's identifying the Israelites of his day with their ancestors at an earlier point in the story of God's dealings with them. (The parable itself, through the characters of the servants and the son, already evokes the *historical* succession of prophets leading up to the Messiah. But the allusion to Isaiah places the parable within the *told* story of God found in the Scriptures.) Jesus is raising the stakes significantly. The Israelites were promised by Moses and the prophets that even though they might be displaced from the land and sent into exile, they would still remain the chosen people. God would continue to watch over them because of his covenant with Abraham, Isaac, and Jacob. But Jesus declares they will no longer enjoy this privileged status. His statement at the end of this parable is amplified by another one reported in Matthew: "many will come from the east and the west [from outside Israel], and will take their places at the feast with Abraham, Isaac and Jacob in the kingdom of heaven. But the subjects of the kingdom [Israelites] will be thrown outside."

Jesus' listeners had no difficulty recognizing where he was placing them within the larger story of God. Matthew records that "when the chief priests and the Pharisees heard Jesus' parables, they knew he was talking about them" and "looked for a way to arrest him." Jesus' method of preaching through stories and pictures was dramatically effective in revealing the intentions of the heart and leading people either to reexamine those intentions, or else embrace to them and turn them into actions.

Many of Jesus' other parables similarly draw on symbolism from the First Testament. Images of obedient and disobedient children, brides and bridegrooms, organic growth in trees and seeds, and other kinds of "figurative symbols" reflect the way the relationship between God

Figure 2.

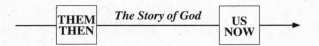

and humanity has been portrayed in the Scriptural *told* story in the years leading up to Jesus. Whether these commonalities constitute deliberate allusions on his part or simply reflect an imagination steeped in the community's storytelling heritage, they have the same effect of situating their hearers within the unfolding story of God.

This approach to preaching arises from, and conveys, a different understanding of the connection between "them then" and "us now" (Figure 2). It's the kind of preaching we will need to cultivate in order to communicate the word of God in postmodernity. Brian McLaren argues that "the Christian message (as we have been telling it)" is now "distant and irrelevant" to "many educated and thoughtful people around the world." Nevertheless, he insists, they still "need to find a larger story in which the stories of their lives can be located."[5] So preaching that situates the story of the listener within the story of God is timely and urgently needed.

It's also thoroughly biblical. As we've seen, it follows the model that Jesus and the apostles provided for us through their own use of the Scriptures that had been written by their time.[6] Preaching this way is biblical in a further sense. It's in keeping with the character of the Scriptures as a collection of literary creations. In fact, it appeals to what they are at their highest level of literary organization. The entire Bible is itself a complex composition. The individual writings within it are set within an overarching framework that structures the whole. As Grelot explains it, everything in the Bible is

> depicted from a particular angle, because the story is truly woven together from the unfolding of God's plan, which is what really underlies the events, characters, and successes and failures of the tiny nation that is looking back at its past. . . . As the biblical narrators undertook to relate the origins of their nation . . . their goal was not to satisfy the curiosity of their contemporaries, but rather to train them in the faith by composing—please excuse the modern terminology—a "catechism" in the form of narratives. As they did this, they would at times include things such as legal codes, practical wisdom teachings, conversations about how God works in the world, and details of the arrangements for the worship of this God.[7]

In other words, the Bible as a whole is built around a framework that is stocked with literary compositions of many types and sizes.[8] The first creation at the beginning of the Bible and the new creation at the end constitute the outer support posts of this framework. The series of covenants that God makes with humanity provide the superstructure in between. These covenants are with Noah, who represents all created life after the flood; with Abraham, Isaac, and Jacob; with the Israelites, through Moses; and with David. The prophets then speak of a "new covenant" that God will make, and this ultimate covenant is established through Jesus Christ. All of the individual writings within the Bible are components of this larger complex composition, and each does its part within it to help tell the story of God. This told story, elaborated over the centuries, creates the connection between "us now" and "them then." As we recognize this, we will pursue a new goal in our preaching. We'll try to enable listeners to see themselves in the story, so they can understand how, as they respond to its retelling, their own stories can become part of it.

Sermons that pursue this goal may take a variety of forms. My intention here is not to argue that non-modern preaching must take on a certain form. I won't try to provide "how-to" instructions for preaching in that form. Rather, I wish to argue that the goal of preaching, in a variety of appropriate forms, should be to situate the story of the listeners within the story of God—not to derive timeless propositions from the text and try to make a connection that way.

This new approach to preaching will require a paradigm shift in what we understand the Bible to be, and a corresponding change in how we read and study the Scriptures. If the task is not to derive timeless doctrines or principles from the text, but rather to situate a story within a story, it's crucial, first of all, for the preacher to understand how a sermon passage functions within a particular book. And this will require, as I've insisted in previous chapters, *reading* to engage the whole composition and then *studying* the parts to understand how they create and receive meaning within it. A presentation of the Scriptures in their natural literary form, which fosters these practices and inhibits contrary ones, is thus an invaluable resource and guide for this new practice of preaching. It helps ensure, for one thing, that the preacher is taking up an appropriate unit that has been situated properly within a literary composition. This is what *The Books of The Bible* has already been doing for those who've been using it for preaching, according to their reports.

A campus staff worker shared how the new habits of Scripture engagement she'd developed by using this edition had changed her approach to the preaching she did from time to time. "When I preached on 'calling' from Ephesians," she wrote, "I read the whole book a few times to get an idea of the context. In the past, I might just have read that chapter, or simply a few verses, importing my own definition of calling and going from there." A young pastor who'd already rejected the approach he described as "propositional preaching" noted similarly, "I try to read through large sections before I preach to get the feel of the passage, and this is certainly made easier with *The Books of The Bible*." When a seminary student praised the new edition in a blog post, someone objected that this might indeed be a "good read-through-the-Bible-in-a-year Bible," but that it wouldn't make "a good preaching Bible." The student countered:

> Actually, I think an edition like this would make a great preaching Bible. It would make a real point to listeners that what matters is the divisions in thought flow, not the divisions of verses. The only kind of preaching for which such a Bible would be

a problem is the kind that scatters itself all over the Bible instead of really explaining one text.

So the presentation in *The Books of The Bible* is already helping preachers, in their sermon preparation, to situate individual episodes, arguments, or oracles within compositions, and to understand how they create and receive meaning in their literary settings.

But the new approach I've been describing requires a further element of preparation. The preacher must also appreciate and be able to explain how a biblical book, and a specific passage within it, helps to tell the ongoing story of God. This will allow listeners to identify with characters and situations in this part of the overall story and find their own place in it. Put simply, preaching this way requires you to *know the story*. And the best way to get to know the story is to read it, all the way through, over and over again. This is where *The Books of The Bible*, as an excellent "read-through-the-Bible" edition, truly does become "a great preaching Bible" as well.

One pastor put it to me this way: "What I see in the Scripture is that Jesus and the disciples were so familiar with the word that when an issue, situation, or circumstance arose out of life, they could speak to it directly using the truth of Scripture. Teaching flowed out of life and out of already knowing the story in general." This pastor expressed his appreciation for how *The Books of The Bible* would encourage continuous reading and thus help people get to know the story better and better. He told me he'd "quit using powerpoint, written notes, etc." for his sermons and was preaching "by just telling story as much as possible."

Another pastor wrote similarly, "*The Books of The Bible* has helped me immerse myself in Scripture again. It's helped reconnect me with the overall message of Scripture. That's impacted my preaching." And a campus minister told me,

> *The Books of the Bible* enables me to do more easily what I've already been doing in my preaching—telling stories, talking about people and sayings and stories. It makes it easier for me to see the stories and people in the Bible. They're fresher in my mind and easier to share. I am a lot more comfortable teaching and leading people through larger, more comprehensive pieces of the Bible—stories, narrative arcs, etc.—than I was before.

A presentation of the Scriptures in their literary form, in other words, lends itself naturally to preaching that seeks to situate a particular Scriptural story within the larger story of God that unfolds throughout the Bible.

It may be objected, however, that many of the compositions in the Bible are not actually "stories." This is quite true. The Scriptures contain writings in a variety of genres, including many non-narrative ones such as law, epistle, genealogy, and poetry. However, even when biblical compositions aren't stories, they still *have* stories. An essential aspect of engaging them as a whole is understanding the story behind them. Why they were written? Under what circumstances? What concerns do they address? Situating *the story of the composition*, whatever its genre, within the unfolding story of God will enable listeners to see how it advances that story and how it can help them find their place within it.

This is one important reason why the biblical books are presented in a new order in *The Books of The Bible*. Related writings are grouped together, and within these groups, works such as Paul's letters and the prophetic books are put in their likely historical order to help demonstrate how the overall *telling of the story* within the Bible unfolds. The introductions to the books explain further when and why they were written. Readers are reporting that these two features of the edition have helped them understand the story of individual books better and also given them the "big picture" of major parts of the Bible. One person wrote, for example:

> Following Paul's letters has always been confusing to me. Even taking classes like New Testament Survey didn't help clarify this. So the background information for each book, coupled with the books being in a more logical order, has really helped me get a more global view of the early days of the church.

In addition to *having* a story, even those biblical books that aren't in the form of stories nevertheless help to *tell* a story. They contribute their own part to the ongoing story of God by attaching themselves to the collection of writings that has already been telling it. They do this by alluding to earlier events, sayings, and symbols. All the Scriptural works are composed within the ongoing life of the covenant community, and at every point in its history, that community finds its bearings by reference to the telling and retelling of the story of its relationship with God. This community, from its earliest days, has always had the

Scriptures in some form, and we see within the Bible that as the community helps to create further inspired works, it orients itself by quotation and allusion to existing ones.

The book of Judges records, for example, that when an angel comes and tells Gideon, "The LORD is with you," he replies, "If the LORD is with us, why has all this happened to us? Where are all his wonders that our ancestors told us about when they said, 'Did not the LORD bring us up out of Egypt?' But now the LORD has abandoned us and given us into the hand of Midian." Gideon knows the story, even though he's only encountered it in oral form. But he can't find his place in it: it's a story of deliverance, while he and his contemporaries are suffering under oppression. With the angel's encouragement and much help from the LORD, however, Gideon is able to write a new chapter in the story and become an agent of deliverance himself. His exploits are then added to the told story, for the benefit of those they will speak to in later generations.

This is evidence from within a biblical narrative that even at a very early stage in the creation of the Scriptures, people in the covenant community oriented themselves by reference and allusion to the story as they knew it in their day. The particular point I'm pursuing here, however, is how this is achieved in non-narrative biblical writings. Both the First and New Testaments provide excellent illustrations of this.

Haggai, for example, speaks this word from God to Zerubbabel, the ruler of Judah after the return from exile: "I will make you like my signet ring, for I have chosen you." This is an intentional allusion to, and direct reversal of, the word that God spoke through Jeremiah to Jehoiachin, who was king before the exile: "Even if you . . . were a signet ring on my right hand, I would still pull you off." These are prophetic oracles, not stories (narratives). But they still *tell* a story, through shared poetic imagery. It's the story of how the people and their ruler had to be judged and, for a time, cast off, but have now been embraced again.

Symbolic connections of this type are pursued much more intensively in the New Testament, as the writers seek to explain and interpret how Jesus has brought the beginnings of the promised new covenant. Through quotations and allusions, these writers show their audience where they fit in the story by drawing connections between elements of life and faith in the multinational community of Jesus' followers, which now constitutes the people of God, and corresponding, prefiguring elements in the history of Israel. These connections are made not just in narrative works, but in all the other New Testament writings as well. To give just one example, at the very beginning of Romans, Paul describes himself as "set apart for the gospel" that God "promised beforehand through his prophets in the Holy Scriptures regarding his Son." Paul is orienting himself and his readers by reference to the told story, specifically the part of it in which the prophets foresee a new covenant. But in his very next phrase, he describes Jesus as a "descendant of David," associating him with God's covenant promises to David as well. These dense allusions and quotations continue throughout the entire epistle.[9]

Thus, in preaching from Romans, while it's crucial to situate individual points within the developing argument of the whole epistle (rather than represent them as timeless propositions), some further steps are needed to help listeners find their place in the story of God. It's necessary both to tell the story of this epistle (how it was created as part of the chapter Paul contributed to the overall story as he became a "light to the Gentiles") and to relate how Paul situates his readers within the larger story of God through his First Testament allusions and quotations. We may not be used to giving much attention to these references in our sermon preparation and preaching. We may feel that they're too complex or confusing for anyone to follow. But the more clearly we can explain them, the more precisely our listeners will be able to situate themselves within the larger story. (One of the best ways to explain allusions like these may be to tell their story as a story. To return to the example from the prophets, "There once was an exiled king named Jehoiachin, who expected that any day he'd be restored to his throne . . .")

As we move from preaching that seeks to derive propositions from the text to preaching that seeks to help listeners find their place in the story of God, the change in aims will likely be felt most keenly and immediately through a new practice in sermons: referencing passages by context and content, rather than by chapter and verse. This is, in fact, the proper practice for non-modern preaching. It's not just that it isn't really possible to navigate by chapters and verses in an edition like *The Books of The Bible*. Preachers *should* reference by content and context, because they're situating a story within a story, and the way we locate ourselves within a story is by referring to its events and overall shape. (One reader of *The Books of The Bible* offered this analogy: "When we watch a movie we never say, 'Oh, scene 3 was great!' We say 'Oh, the part where he . . . was great!' What if we talked about the Bible like that?")

Those who have been conditioned by modernity to expect fast, easy access to the Bible through chapters and verses might well wonder how referencing by context and content could ever work. They should consider, however, that the Bible itself models this kind of referencing. Jesus and the apostles had no chapters or verses to navigate by, but they were able to indicate precise passages within the Scriptures anyway. Mark records, for example, that when Jesus was debating with the Sadducees about the resurrection, he referred to a particular Scripture passage by asking, "Have you not read in the Book of Moses, in the account of the burning bush . . . ?" Even though this isn't even a reference to a specific book (but rather to the whole Torah), the passage is readily identifiable. Indeed, the New Testament writers were able to synthesize and communicate a comprehensive new interpretation of the First Testament Scriptures without relying on any chapter and verse numbers at all. So the problem isn't that referencing by content and context is simply impractical.

Rather, the problem is biblical illiteracy. If we protest that we could never find things in the Bible by content and context, we're basically admitting that we just don't know the Bible well enough to do so. And this may well be the case. Glenn Paauw wrote a post about "Organic References" for *The Books of The Bible Blog*,[10] encouraging people to refer to

Scripture passages "in natural, contextual, literary ways." A pastor responded on his own blog, saying, "I completely agree. The more context, both historical and literary, that can be provided in a sermon or study the better. People need to know where the stories are coming from, why they are where they are, etc." But a reader warned in reply, "In any given church, if you said, 'Turn in the book of 1 Kings to the story of Elijah and the prophets of Baal,' pages would be rustling for minutes. Some people would never find it. And that's not good." No, it isn't. But the problem isn't with the method of referencing by content and context. It's with the low level of Bible literacy that makes people helpless to use it.

What's responsible for this biblical illiteracy? For one thing, our current Bible practices, such as reading only small selections at a time. These practices haven't helped people become broadly familiar with the Scriptures. Referencing by chapter and verse is also to blame, because it allows people to find passages without ever learning where they fit. (People end up like the character of Kerry in Brian McLaren's book *The Story We Find Ourselves In*, who admits, "I heard all kinds of Bible stories as a kid, but I have no idea how they fit together—which comes first, that sort of thing. To me, they're just isolated episodes in a larger story I never really understood."[11]) And our concept of what the Bible is probably also contributes significantly to the problem. If the Bible is essentially a source of propositions, or a compendium of devotional passages, then there's really no need to appreciate the sweep of an overall story, and to place events and stories within it. As one reader of *The Books of The Bible* put it,

> The format of our Bibles is a large disservice in understanding the theology of the biblical story. It is too easy to see scriptures as separate, unconnected segments or propositions. To some degree this segmentation has aided a modernistic and moralistic approach to the biblical texts; this is not the intention of the authors, and this reading approach has sadly made many of us put our Bibles down more often than we have been engaged by and in the story.

We need to come to a new understanding of what the Scriptures are, and we need to reflect this understanding in new presentations and practices, especially "reading" as it was described in Chapter 4. Adopting the discipline of referencing by content and context, rather than by chapters and verses, will foster these new understandings and approaches. This practice will become more comfortable, meaningful, and natural as biblical literacy increases. It can then serve as an effective tool within non-modern preaching.[12]

The presentation of the biblical writings in *The Books of The Bible* is already helping to bring about these changes. One reader of the edition noted in his blog that using it called for "a new intellectual grid based not on numbers but ideas. I had to navigate the Bible the way I would another book, by knowing the content, not the references. Now that really could change the way you view Scripture." Another observed, "I think my biblical literacy is actually increasing in the absence of verse and chapter markers." And at least one pastor is already referencing by content and context, rather than by the numerical grid. He admits, "I know a lot of Scripture by heart, but I rarely can tell you chapter or verse." He tells the people in his church "to read the books as a whole so often that they are familiar with the points of the stories, the parables, and the teachings." Reports like these show how people are already preaching "after chapters and verses," helping people to understand the story and to see how their own stories are part of it.

Chapter Seven
Teaching the Bible after Chapters & Verses:
Inviting People to Join the Conversation

A youth pastor warns in a recent blog post that "to-day's church must rethink its structural set up" if it doesn't want to lose the "upcoming generations." By "set up" he means specifically the size, shape, furnishing, and arrangement of the rooms where meetings for youth and young adults are held. But his ultimate interest is in the kind of interactions that various setups permit or prevent. Most of the time, he notes, both in school and in church, young people are "taught at" and "spoken to" because the physical configuration is, "Teacher in the front of the classroom, instilling knowledge and facts to silent students all sitting in rows." "Where," he wonders, "is the dialog, interaction, and participation?" He doubts that "to-day's students . . . learn best in a stagnant, uncreative, and individualistic environment."[1] Note that individualism, a cherished value of modernity, is now associated with being "stagnant" and "uncreative"! And so this youth pastor recommends, as an appropriate model, the physical arrangements and teaching approach he saw on a visit to Solomon's Porch in Minneapolis:

> Plenty of couches and chairs in a circular pattern. The speaker, Doug Pagitt, sits on a stool in the center and makes himself, and his message, very approachable during the teaching times. People are encouraged to interact with the message, ask questions, and be creative and conversational in their response. And, probably most importantly, is that everyone is humanized. They sit in a way that looks the other person in the eye and promotes physical contact and touch.

This writer's argument, in other words, is that postmodern people learn best interactively, through dialogue and conversation, and that all the arrangements we make for teaching should promote this approach.

(The mention of Doug Pagitt raises an important issue. He has argued that conversational teaching should replace monological preaching within Christian worship.[2] I'm arguing in this book, however, that "after chapters and verses" there will still be a place for both preaching the Bible and teaching the Bible, as separate activities. I'll come back to this concern later in this chapter.)

Other reflections on teaching the Bible in a postmodern context similarly stress dialogue and conversation. In a blog post on how to lead a Bible study with "today's teens," a self-described next-generation church planter writes, "It is vitally important that interactive and experiential methods are used. . . . Postmodern teens do not just want to sit and listen to someone else talk."[3] (Interestingly, in light of our earlier discussions in this book, this post also advises, "Wrap the entire lesson around a single scripture passage if at all possible. Using a large number of additional verses that are not part of the main text is actually counter-productive.") The same emphases are found in materials on "Teaching the Bible in Challenging Times" developed by Focus, a British media ministry, to help pastors, teachers, and small group leaders present the Scriptures more effectively to "postmodern people." These materials encourage leaders to ask in their preparations, "What can I do to make my teaching interactive and open to question?"[4] (To touch on our earlier discussions once again, these materials similarly advise leaders to "teach through whole books" and "follow the Bible's own natural units of thought.")

Recommendations like these are sails in the wind, indicating in which direction it's carrying us across a cultural divide. They all illustrate what teaching, and specifically Bible teaching, will need to look like in postmodernity. Modern teaching was a transfer of information—abstract, objective knowledge—from teacher to students. When modern teachers entertained questions, this was typically to help listeners understand better what they were telling them. But postmodern teachers expect that students' questions will likely help them understand things better themselves. They have some of the picture, but students have other parts that they need to contribute as the group works things out together.

I pastored churches near colleges and universities for nearly twenty years, and I continue to serve as a volunteer staff member with a national campus ministry. As a result,

I've had many opportunities to help with student Bible studies. Over the past two decades I've seen a definite change in the students' expectations of me. Originally they wanted me to teach the lessons myself, though they appreciated having the opportunity to ask clarifying questions during and after each session. In more recent years the students have preferred to rotate the actual leadership of the study among themselves. And there isn't really a "lesson." The group reads a passage together and the leader writes down everyone's comments, questions, and observations. They then talk these over one at a time. My role is usually to serve as a resource, to help facilitate a student-run discussion. I've even been asked to let the conversation play out for a while before addressing subjects I might be knowledgeable about. "Don't speak up right away," a student leader told me. "We want people to wrestle with things together first." In postmodernity, the value is not on getting information quickly and efficiently, but on the community exploring shared questions together.

I still lead studies myself from time to time, and when I do, my experiences continue to underscore how much things have changed. On one occasion I realized that the lesson plan I'd prepared and followed during the study had really constrained the discussion, even though I plugged in all the questions the group had raised when they first read the passage. "They don't want me to answer their questions in the course of talking about the passage," I said to myself afterward. "They want me to talk about the passage in the course of answering their questions." This is because, in the postmodern context, truth is engaged through the medium of the participants' experience and their reflections on it. We were there to engage the word of God. But what gave us access to it, in the group's implicit understanding, was not primarily our reason or knowledge, but the impact its truths were having on our experience and on the experience of other people in our lives.

This isn't to say that there's no lesson to be taught, no plan to be followed anymore. But it needs to be followed flexibly and perhaps nonsequentially. The idea is for the "teacher" to bring their prepared lesson to the conversation, rather than bringing the conversation to it.

This collaborative approach to exploring the Scriptures was highlighted visually for me when I visited what would probably have been called an "investigative Bible study" not too many years ago. In this case it was called a "dialogue." The group met on a university campus, and it included both students and professors. It was described as an opportunity to "engage in an open, respectful and thoughtful dialogue about the Bible and life." The chairs were set in a couple of rows in a circular pattern. The passage of Scripture that served as the basis of the evening's discussion was projected from the leader's laptop computer onto a screen that he stood by. As participants asked questions or made observations, the leader would record them all around the passage using an electronic stylus, so that they appeared on the screen too—a postmodern gloss. By the time we were done, we had before us a visual representation of how reflections in response to the Bible that arise from personal experience now provide the medium through which it is accessed.

The kind of teaching that postmodernity invites and requires actually corresponds much more closely to the true character of the Scriptures than teaching which, either in its physical form or in the way it is conducted, represents "teacher in the front of the classroom, instilling knowledge and facts to silent students all sitting in rows." The Bible is not a systematic description of the ways and deeds of God, communicated from a single perspective. In the Bible, no sooner is one part of the story of God told, from one point of view, than it's retold from a different one. "This is what I saw," says one writer, "and this is what I believe it means." "I saw it this way," responds another, "and I believe it means this." The Scriptures aren't an exposition. They're a conversation.

The clearest example of this is the way the Bible presents not one but four accounts of the life of Jesus. While the overall outlines of the story are much the same in each gospel, the various writers make their own cases for what the life, death, and resurrection of Jesus mean by selecting their materials differently and then arranging them differently. John tells almost the entire story of Jesus from a Judean perspective, even though Jesus carried out most of his ministry in Galilee. Episodes in Jesus' life are put in various orders, and related at varying lengths. (For example, the baptism of Jesus, accorded great significance in the other gospels, is mentioned only in passing by Luke, in a subordinate, circumstantial clause: "When all the people had been baptized, *Jesus having been baptized* and praying, the heavens opened . . ."[5]) Some sayings and speeches are recorded in one gospel but not in others. And even when two or more gospel writers include the same saying, it may be related in one context by one writer but in a different context by another, who is effectively giving it a different application.

A great number of individual differences like these could be listed, but what's even more important is the overall effect. Each writer is giving his own inspired perspective on Jesus' life. Recognizing this, the church has traditionally associated the four gospels with the four living creatures in the visions of Ezekiel and in Revelation: the lion, the eagle, the ox, and the man. Four separate beings are telling us about Jesus as they see him.

Multiple perspectives are also brought in as other parts of the story of God are told. The First Testament presents two sprawling histories of the Israelite nation, Samuel–Kings and Chronicles–Ezra–Nehemiah. Once again, the two literary creations reflect different understandings of how the story should be told, and thus of the story itself. Samuel–Kings traces the monarchy from its beginning, when the last judge (Samuel) anointed the first king (Saul), to its end in the Babylonian exile. Chronicles–Ezra–Nehemiah begins its story all the way back at Adam, and ends it with the return from exile and the restoration of the people's institutions. Along the way, different selections are made of what materials to include. Samuel–Kings describes the reigns of monarchs in both the northern and southern kingdoms (Israel and Judah). Chronicles–Ezra–Nehemiah considers only the Judean rulers. And it completely omits David's sin against Bathsheba and Uriah. Samuel–Kings, by contrast, gives extended attention to this episode and its later consequences, as the nation was plunged into civil war.

The entire New Testament may be understood as a reflection on how the coming of Jesus has cast the story of God up to that point in a new light. Through Jesus, God has revealed that events, celebrations and institutions in the life of Israel have a deeper meaning than appears on their surface. But what exactly is their meaning? The New Testament writers express a variety of perspectives. We saw in Chapter 2 that for Paul, the true temple is the community of Jesus' followers, while for the writer of Hebrews, the true temple is heavenly, "not made with human hands." John sees things from a third perspective. He considers the true temple to be the body of Jesus. According to John, when Jesus said, "Destroy this temple, and I will raise it again in three days," "the temple he had spoken of was his body." These are not contradictory perspectives. They're complementary. But they are different, and sitting side by side in the pages of the New Testament, they're in conversation.

Multiple perspectives are offered on other questions of how Jesus' followers are to understand and live out the new in light of the old. Jesus said, for instance, "Nothing outside you can defile you by going into you. Rather, it is what comes out of you that defiles you." What are the implications of this statement? According to Mark, "In saying this, Jesus declared all foods clean." But according to Matthew, the implications are that "eating with unwashed hands does not defile you." In Matthew, Mark, and Luke,

Jesus defends his work of healing on the Sabbath by arguing that it's a day on which it's "lawful" to "do good." But in
John, Jesus explains that *he* isn't working on the Sabbath;
his Father is working, and it's his Father's work that he's
doing. In Hebrews, by contrast, entering into the Sabbath-
rest of God means ceasing from one's own labor as God
ceased from his (God *hasn't* been working?), and this
means living in faith and obedience rather than in unbelief
and disobedience.

As biblical authors express different perspectives on
the meaning and significance of the story of God, they may
even engage other authors intentionally. Job, for example,
seems to be making direct reference to Psalm 8 when he
protests to God, "What are human beings that you make so
much of them, that you give them so much attention?" For
David, who wrote this psalm, God's continual watchfulness
was a source of comfort and security. For Job, it's oppressive scrutiny. There are two ways to look at it, the book of
Job is saying.

Many other examples could be given of how biblical
writers express multiple perspectives, but the interactive
character of the Scriptural writings should be evident by
now. I will therefore conclude with just one more example,
from Proverbs. In Solomon's collection of sayings, these
two proverbs are placed right next to one another:

> Do not answer fools according to their folly,
> or you yourself will be just like them.

> Answer fools according to their folly,
> or they will be wise in their own eyes.

Anyone who's looking for the "right answer" to the question, "What do I do when I'm talking to a fool?" is going to be disappointed and frustrated here. "Well, which one is it?" they'll demand to know. But this juxtaposition of different perspectives on what to do in this case actually provides a *more comprehensive view* of the question. In this way the collection of wisdom sayings in Proverbs is a microcosm of the whole Bible: it too pulls together different perspectives, putting them in conversation with one another. This provides a more comprehensive view of the epochal redemptive-historical events the Bible relates than any single perspective could. These events are so significant and evocative that only multiple perspectives can do them justice. Indeed, the more important the event, the more perspectives it needs to be seen from. Thus the culminating events of the life, death, and resurrection of Jesus are seen from the greatest number of perspectives of all.

This recognition of the conversational character of the Scriptures helps answer a question that was raised earlier in this chapter. Why should there still be preaching? Why should the followers of Jesus ever be "taught at" and "spoken to" when they gather to worship and are seeking to hear the word of God? Why shouldn't the format instead be "dialog, interaction, and participation" (as people like Doug Pagitt have modeled and advocated)? The answer I would offer is that preaching, as described in the previous chapter, is essentially telling a story so that the listeners can find their place in it. And when someone is telling a story, it's not really suitable to have other people talking at the same time. Indeed, storytellers typically address any interruptions, questions, or objections by saying, "Wait till you've heard the whole story."

But I would define teaching within the community of Jesus' followers as something different. I'd say it's the opportunity we have to invite people to join in the conversation that's begun in the pages of Scripture and continues down through our day. It's important and necessary both to give people the chance to hear the story so they can recognize their place in it and to talk about the meaning of the story with others who are also part of it. Teaching takes the work that's done in reading, studying, and preaching—appreciating a whole literary creation, its parts, and its place in the story—and puts it into play within the web of relationships in the community.

The Bible itself models for us this combination of proclamation and conversation (monologue and dialogue) in different kinds of community gatherings. Acts, for example, records many of Paul's sermons and speeches. But it also records that when Paul visited the believers in Troas on his way to Jerusalem, he "dialogued"[6] with them all night. Jesus himself would speak publicly to the crowds, but also interact with his disciples more privately, answering their questions and clarifying his message for them.

A similar pattern has typically characterized life in local communities of Jesus' followers. One British reviewer of Pagitt's book, appreciating its emphases but advocating for a combination of preaching and teaching within the church, recalled the historic practices of his own tradition:

In the earliest Baptist communities, three or more

members would preach when the people gathered—but each sermon would be monological. Why? I think because they instinctively grasped that the monologue is uniquely powerful to address the emotions, and so to challenge for change. The preachers, week by week, would call the people to repentance and conversion, to a desire to re-align their lives with the gospel of Christ. Then, in "progressive conversations" that took place elsewhere in the life of the church, that desire could be nurtured and realised.[7]

I share this vision of different practices being used in different settings to achieve complementary purposes, and so I would still call the conversational/dialogical approach we've been considering in this chapter "teaching," and consider it distinct from "preaching." I'd argue that there's a place in one part of the community's life for preaching and a place in another part of it for teaching.

Preaching is less interactive. It's proclamational; it tells the story. Because it takes place within a worship setting, it's entitled to assume that its listeners are either believers or honest seekers who will give reverent attention and not express immediate opposition. (Respect for the beliefs and practices of others dictates that we don't go to any religious group's worship gathering to be disruptive or antagonistic.) At the same time, even if preaching is less interactive, preachers should always be informed by, and seek to address, the situation and concerns of the people in their community. A sermon shouldn't be a lecture or a reprimand from someone you don't know. It won't be, if the preacher is sharing with the people, bringing them along, inviting them in. The more preachers can be transparent about their own questions, feelings, and experiences, the more genuinely the listeners will "know" them, even if they aren't well acquainted personally.[8]

Teaching, on the other hand, is more interactive, much more shaped by students' questions, observations, and concerns. While, like preaching, it intends to influence, it does this by imparting an understanding that will work its effects more gradually, over time. Teaching typically takes place in a religiously neutral setting: even within church buildings, there are classrooms for teaching; classes aren't usually held in the sanctuary. In this neutral setting, all ideas have to hold their own; none are privileged in the discussion because they are tenets of the faith. (Otherwise, what's happening isn't teaching, but indoctrination.) Give-and-take, "push back," is not just permissible, but desirable. Teaching lends itself more to questions, comments, challenges, exploration. It's a guided conversation. And in the postmodern context, it's expected that greater comprehension, and more of the truth, will emerge specifically through this dialogical process.

How can a new understanding of what the Bible is, embodied in our presentations and practices, make teaching the Scriptures more effective in postmodernity? How can it help those in the rising generations want to engage the Bible in the years ahead?

Some years after Watchman Nee had written *The Spiritual Man*, he rethought the approach he'd taken in that book. He concluded that the "headings, the orderliness, the systematic way in which the subject is worked out, the logic of the argument" were "all too perfect to be spiritual." His goal, he explained, had been to leave his readers with no unanswered questions at the end of the book. "But God, I have discovered, does not do things that way." "Much less does He let us do them," Nee continued. "If God gives us books they will ever be broken fragments, not always clear or consistent or logical, lacking conclusions, and yet coming to us in life and ministering life to us. We cannot dissect divine facts and outline and systematize them." Nee noted that this was the "fundamental character" of "the Word of God itself": "it speaks always and essentially to our spirit and to our life."[9] In other words, the Bible does not make a systematized appeal to the rational faculties, but presents the whole person with "broken fragments" whose meaning is explored as they're tentatively and partially pieced together in community. (The literary compositions in the Scriptures, I would note, are complete and beautiful in themselves, but they are shaped in such varying ways that they can't be fit together neatly into a systematic-theological edifice. In that sense they are "broken fragments" of an elusive comprehensive system.)

Modern formats and uses of the Bible, however, suggest that it has a very different character. When placed within the grid of a fixed book order and numbered chapter and verse divisions, the Scriptures appear to have been analyzed, systematized, solved. The grid asserts that everything does fit together in an orderly way. There are no gaps, nothing's out of line. The meaningful statements

have been isolated and cataloged, and they can be con-
nected to one another through cross-reference systems.

Indeed, since statements in the Bible are labeled and
numbered, its contents appear to have a legal character.
And appealing to legal authority is a way of shutting down
conversation rather than opening it up. Asking, for example,
how to balance the interests of gun owners with a concern
for community safety makes for a wide-ranging and impas-
sioned conversation. But if a person addresses the issue
by insisting that their "second amendment rights" (as they
understand them) allow them to keep doing exactly what
they've been doing, there's nothing to discuss. In the same
way, an appeal to "book, chapter, and verse" that takes you
directly to a "controlling legal authority" implies that this
particular question of belief or practice has been settled
beyond debate.

Another aspect of the modern format, the section
headings that have been introduced by translators and
publishers, may also have the unintended effect of
presenting the Scriptures as something whose meaning
has been resolved. They don't suggest that the biblical
writings are documents whose meaning remains to be
explored and stays open even after much investigation.
Section headings represent *conclusions*. "This is what
this passage is about," they imply. They don't invite you
to "see what you can discover." One young man, in a blog
post, compared reading a Bible with section headings
to "watching a film with someone leaning over every
thirty seconds to pseudo-whisper, 'Psst! This is the part
where . . .'" He said he was grateful for the way *The Books*

of The Bible had removed section headings. Continuing the cinematic analogy, he stated, "I feel like maybe, just maybe, taking the film in on the director's terms for the first few times will be sufficient."

Modern Bible teaching methods reinforce the impression that modern presentations create—that the Scriptures are a storehouse of established facts and right answers that can be retrieved at the proper coordinates. Many study guides, for example, instruct students to look up information and fill in the blanks in their workbooks. Or in an electronic variation, the teacher will have a PowerPoint chart up on the screen and pop the right answer into each box once the class has successfully given it. In general, modern Bible teaching resources are shaped by the assumption that the task of the teacher is to convey information for students to retain. New presentations and practices are needed for the postmodern world that will represent teaching instead as guiding a conversation that continues the one begun in the Scriptures.

This is the vision we express in the preface to *The Books of The Bible*. We explain that our goal in making significant format changes was to "help readers enjoy their encounter with the sacred text and to read with more understanding, so that they may take their places more readily within this story of new creation." We then explain how we "encourage readers to study the Bible in community."[10] In other words, we look for our place in the story, and we talk about the story with others who are part of it. In keeping with this vision, many features of *The Books of The Bible* help remove the imprint of modernity from the Scriptures, allowing them to be taught more effectively in an interactive community context.

For one thing, changing the order of the books effectively breaks up the single-volume Bible of modernity. As I explained in Chapter 3, our goal in making this change was not to try to create the best possible new sequence to displace the existing one, but rather to return to the fluidity of book order that prevailed for the first three quarters of the full Bible's history. (The particular order we used did reflect certain designs; these included grouping books together that arose within the same stream of reflection on the story of God. This, in itself, indicates that the Bible is a conversation, since there are different streams within it. But the ultimate goal was to free the biblical books to be arranged in a variety of suitable ways.) The Bible is not a monolithic treatise. The book names aren't the first level of indexing for its contents. The Bible is instead a collection of individual books, and these can be arranged in a number of ways. They may be put in different positions relative to one another depending on the goals of the presentation. All of this means that the Scriptural writings really are in conversation with one another. (Publishing individual books separately, as Biblica has already done for Psalms, Amos, Ecclesiastes, John, and Luke–Acts in *The Books of The Bible* format, demonstrates even more clearly that the Scriptures are a library of writings that offer multiple perspectives on the story of God.)

Some users of the edition have recognized the goal of the departure from the traditional book order and appreciated its effects. The new order met with a few strong reactions, suggesting that some people, in their under-standing of what the Bible is and their beliefs about how it came to have its present form, attach a high degree of authority to a fixed, traditional order. "Bibles have this," they're effectively insisting. For example, one person who reviewed *The Books of The Bible* very favorably on his blog specified that his "only quibble" was that "the books are not in canonical order." Another person who commented on a different blog's review of the edition similarly asserted the authority of tradition in support of the usual order. He asked whether we editors thought we were "somehow superior compilers than the original communities that formed the canon." But another person responded, quite accurately, "I think the main point of reordering the books is to: 1. Show the interconnection of various books to help readers see the historical and theological connections; 2. Show that there is no 'correct' order of the books of the Bible." Indeed, there is not. And when the biblical books are freed from their accustomed settings in a monolithic volume, their individual voices, their contributions to the conversation, are heard much more clearly. One reader reported, "When the gospels were grouped together, each gospel lost any distinguishing features in my mind. This new grouping helps me to differentiate the gospels." Another reader noted similarly that the new order "broadens your perspective to include the particular distinctiveness of the authors' voices."

A second feature of *The Books of The Bible* that pro-motes an interactive, conversational approach to teaching the Scriptures is the removal of section headings. These headings, as we've noted, supply a conclusion in advance about what a passage is saying. Reaching any different conclusion requires challenging a judgment that's been embedded right into the text of the Bible. But when there are no headings, students have greater freedom and encouragement to work out their own understandings. One user offered this analogy in a comment on *The Books of The Bible Blog*:

> Back in high school or university, if you were a student who could not afford new textbooks, you would likely scramble for the least marked-up, most "unadulterated" versions in the used section. You'd want to get the most pristine copy. You would very likely loathe the thought of having to face some previous student's distracting markups and notes all year, most of which were out of context with your own comprehension of the subject matter. With a clean(er) copy, you'd be free to annotate your own interpretation and thoughts on what you were studying (and still consult with others).

One further feature of *The Books of The Bible* that may subtly encourage people to contribute their own voices to the conversation in its pages is the use of white space, of varying widths, to mark off literary sections of different levels. As I've already noted, while this spacing arguably also represents a conclusion (about how a literary work is put together), it's not so assertive a conclusion as putting things in writing would be. Indeed, the reticence of this approach, by contrast with labeling and captioning, may constitute, for some, a visual invitation to add their own voice. "There's room for you in this conversation," the open space says. This is admittedly not the original purpose of this feature. But it may be a welcome, even if unintended, consequence. One reader reported that without "all the clutter on the pages," "I am greeted by a silence on the page as I read, a silence that helps me hear the whisper of the Holy Spirit." The silence is also an invitation to whisper back.

However, the most important feature of the edition for encouraging interactive, dialogical teaching of the Bible is also the one whose practical implications people have wondered about the most: the absence of chapter and verse numbers. Let's re-examine the hypothetical situation we considered in Chapter 6 and ask some further questions about it. The leader asks everyone to "turn in the book of 1 Kings to the story of Elijah and the prophets of Baal." Pages are "rustling for minutes," but some people still never find it. How should we respond to this situation? Must we either put the chapter and verse numbers back in, or else accept that some people are just going to be lost by the wayside?

Why do we frame the choices in this way? Are we so conditioned by the modern premium on speed and information that we can only think of two alternatives: trying to find our way around in a treasury of great literature by using a numerical index, or leaving people lost and confused without one? How about *interacting* with them, as we all find our place together? Isn't it a good thing that, with *The Books of The Bible*, simply getting to the passage you want to talk about may require a conversation? Being able to reference by chapters and verses means that you don't need to bring people along with you on a journey to the passage within the Scriptures. That's a significant loss for their knowledge of the story of God, and an opportunity missed for getting a great start on a conversation that will continue the one that takes place within the Bible around the story.

We need to change the picture we have in our minds, which has been inspired by modernity, where the person up front with all the knowledge fires off references in the course of an information transfer and we impose a numerical grid on our Bibles to help as many people as possible keep up as best they can. Let's replace that picture with one in which the leader patiently and observantly draws on the group's own experience of the Scriptural writings to guide them into the passage they'll be discussing together. We don't have to get there as fast as possible so that the teaching can begin. It's already begun.

In a post to *The Books of The Bible Blog*, I provided an illustration of how this might work. The example I gave was in the context of preaching; the interaction could be even richer in teaching. I suggested that instead of announcing the Scripture lesson as "Matthew 6:5–15," a pastor could explain that the message would be based on "Jesus' discussion of prayer in the Sermon on the Mount." And the pastor, looking out over the congregation to track their progress, could guide them in this way:

> Has everybody found Matthew? Good. Now Matthew begins with the genealogy of Jesus, then the story of his birth and early ministry. Flip

through those, and you'll come to a collection of his foundational teachings. There Jesus first tells us what it means to be blessed; then he tells us how we can truly fulfill the law; and then he tells us in what spirit we should give and pray and fast. We're going to look this morning at what he says about prayer. Does everybody have the place?[11]

Not only do they have the place, they see how Matthew tells the story of Jesus, and they recognize where the passage they'll be looking at fits within the story. It's not just an "isolated episode."

In a teaching context, students themselves could help guide their group to a passage. If, in the course of an evening's discussion, people wanted to bring up other Scriptures that they thought would make a helpful contribution, they could explain to the others where and how to find them, so everyone could look at them together. No chapters and verses needed. Just patience, and a recognition that walking together to a destination within the story of God is time well spent. As Peter Enns writes,

> Perhaps we should think of biblical interpretation more as a path to walk than a fortress to be defended. . . . The burden of "getting it right" can sometimes be discouraging and hinder effective ministry. I would rather think of biblical interpretation as a path we walk, a pilgrimage we take, whereby the longer we walk and take in the surrounding scenes, the more people we stop and converse with along the way, the richer our interpretation will be.[12]

Conclusion

I n the centuries after Michelangelo painted his mag-
nificent frescoes on the ceiling of the Sistine Chapel,[1]
those frescoes were covered with several successive
layers of varnish. This varnish originally had a positive
purpose: it was applied to preserve the paintings. In time
it darkened, however, creating a brown patina that was
deepened by coatings of soot and smoke from candles in
the chapel. This superimposed effect conditioned how the
artwork was experienced and understood in the centuries
that followed. Its original appearance was lost to cultural
memory. But as the chapel was being cleaned in major
restoration project (finally completed in 1999 after twenty
years), it was discovered that Michelangelo's original col-
ors had actually been very bright and bold. The "beauty
behind the mask" was visible once again, and his frescoes
could be appreciated with something much closer to the
effect he had intended.

The Bible, as I've insisted throughout this book, is also
a work of elegant beauty. The writings within it possess a
beauty of form and expression that is meant to attract us to

the truth it presents. As Julie Ackerman Link writes, God doesn't expect truth to "stand alone." "God," she writes, "adorns truth with beauty and goodness, making it into something that appeals to every aspect of our being— our hearts and souls and bodies as well as our minds."[2] Unfortunately, over the centuries, and particularly in modernity, the Bible has been reshaped, so that we now see different forms in the pages of Scripture—unattractive ones, which don't draw us to the truth in the Bible. Our experience of Bible reading is thus far less satisfying and fulfilling, and far less effective in deepening our relationship with God, than it should be.

While the parallels between the Sistine Chapel restoration and the task of uncovering the songs, stories, poems and dreams within the Bible should be evident, this is nevertheless an imperfect analogy. The forms in Michaelangelo's frescoes could still be recognized behind the patina, while the Bible's literary creations have been not just darkened, but distorted. An even more suitable analogy to the effect that the historical reshaping has on our appreciation for Scripture may therefore be to a work of glorious architecture that scaffolding has been put around to permit repairs or to provide structural support. These are positive purposes. But the scaffolding unfortunately also creates a geometric grid that guides the eye around the building, directing the attention away from its architectural beauties to a mere caricature of its proportions and harmonies. And even this analogy is a limited one, since the Bible is in no need of repair, and it can stand perfectly well on its own. The scaffolding that's been put up around the biblical text can be quite safely dismantled.

That's what I hope will happen in the years ahead, through new presentations like *The Books of The Bible* and through the new practices of reading, studying, preaching, and teaching the Scriptures that these presentations will permit and encourage. It would be a great shame if the beautiful and powerful literary creations within the Bible continued to be so badly obscured. But there's a lot more than this at stake. Entire future generations may cease to listen to the word of God if we continue to present and use it in such a distorted form. Those of us who've gotten to know the Bible in its modern shape will need to step out of our comfort zones, take some risks, unlearn some old habits, and learn some new ones if we want to help develop presentations and practices that will communicate meaningfully to these generations. This is the challenge of our time. We need to stop hugging the comfortable shoreline of our accustomed approaches to the Bible. Jesus is saying to us, as he did to Peter when he first met him, "Push out into the deep water." I'll meet you out there.

Notes

Introduction

1. The Center for Bible Engagement, "Why?" www.centerforbibleengagement.org.

2. David Kinnaman, "The Bible and the Next Generation: A Snapshot of the American Context for Bible Engagement," paper delivered to American Bible Society "Scriptorium" consultation, Houston, March 25–26, 2009.

3. "Older people are more likely to read the Bible than are younger people. Fifty percent of those over the age of 65 read the Bible at least weekly, compared to 27% of people between the ages of 18 and 29." Alec Gallup and Wendy W. Simmons, "Six in Ten Americans Read Bible at Least Occasionally," *Gallup News Service*, October 20, 2000. http://www.gallup.com/poll/2416/Six-Ten-Americans-Read-Bible-Least-Occasionally.aspx.

4. In Chapter 3 I'll note some additional factors that are also contributing to the decline in biblical literacy. But throughout this book I'll be arguing that our changing culture's increasing disaffection with "modern" presentations and practices is an extremely significant factor that we must address.

5. Stephen Joel Garver, "Emerging in Postmodernity," *Sacra Doctrina*, December 5, 2006. http://sacradoctrina.blogspot.com/2006_12_05_archive.html.

6. Donald Miller, *Searching for God Knows What* (Nashville: Thomas Nelson, 2004), 152.

7. Indeed, most of the Bible was composed orally and intended to be delivered orally, so written, printed, and electronic presentations are all at least one step away from the original form. In Chapter 4 I will discuss ways in which the "new orality" of postmodernity can help recapture this original feature of the Bible.

8. Richard Moulton, ed., *The Modern Reader's Bible* (New York and London: Macmillan, 1907), v.

9. Brian McLaren, *A New Kind of Christian* (San Francisco: Jossey-Bass, 2001), 158.

10. "Inventing 'The Bible': Revelation, Theology, Phenomenon, and Text," http://www.joelgarver.com/writ/phil/bible.htm. Garver also discusses how "theological categories for explaining the Scriptures . . . shifted . . . so that revelation [became] more an extrinsic super-addition of information into the created order" and how the "Scriptures came to be treated less as a self-manifestation of God" and "more an object of critical study." These are vital matters relating to the wider issue of Bible practices. But our immediate concern here is with an understanding of what the Bible is, as expressed in physical presentations and devotional uses.

11. I'll offer a fuller discussion in Chapter 1 of how chapters and verses were introduced to the Bible, and I'll explain more about book order in Chapter 2.

12. Stanley Grenz and John Francke, *Beyond Foundationalism: Shaping Theology in a Postmodern Context* (Louisville: Westminster John Knox, 2001), 13. These authors are actually describing the perspective toward the Bible of "the rationalist approach that typifies evangelical theology." But the modern shaping of the Scriptures encourages and fosters this perspective.

13. http://www.youtube.com/watch?v=nsDEvR4iijQ.

14. Michelle P. Brown, online catalog, "In the Beginning: Bibles Before the Year 1000," Smithsonian Institution, Freer Gallery of Art, http://www.asia.si.edu/exhibitions/online/ITB/html/introduction.htm.

Chapter One

1. Ersnt Würthwein, *The Text of the Old Testament*, trans. Erroll F. Rhodes (Grand Rapids: Eerdmans, 1995), 20.

2. Robert H. Pfeiffer, *Introduction to the Old Testament* (New York: Harper and Brothers, 1948), 81.

3. See Kurt Aland and Barbara Aland, *The Text of the New Testament*, 2nd ed., tr. Erroll F. Rhodes (Grand Rapids: Eerdmans and Leiden: E.J. Brill, 1989), 252ff.

4. Ibid., 80.

5. Gordon D. Fee and Douglas Stuart, *How to Read the Bible For All Its Worth* (Grand Rapids: Zondervan, 1982), 20.

6. Christopher R. Smith, "The Literary Structure of Leviticus," *Journal for the Study of the Old Testament* 70 (1996): 17–32.

7. Christopher R. Smith, "Literary Evidences of a Fivefold Structure in the Gospel of Matthew," *New Testament Studies* 43 (1997): 540–51.

8. Grant Osborne, *The Hermeneutical Spiral: A Comprehensive Introduction to Biblical Interpretation* (Downers Grove, IL: InterVarsity Press, 1991), 23.

9. Kay Arthur, *How to Study Your Bible: The Lasting Rewards of the Inductive Approach* (Eugene, OR: Harvest House, 1994), 40.

10. Ibid., 53. However, Arthur also encourages readers to study a book of the Bible chapter by chapter and to write chapter summaries. It seems more consistent with her own stated goals and methods to invite her readers instead to discern "subsegments," between "segments" and "paragraphs," and to study these in place of chapters.

Chapter Two

1. Luke Timothy Johnson, *The Gospel of Luke*, Sacra Pagina 3 (Collegeville, MN: Liturgical Press, 1991), 14–15.

2. According to Liddell and Scott, the term *logos* was used to refer to one section of a historical work; in the plural, it meant a full "chronicle" or an ordered collection of such historical accounts. *Greek-English Lexicon* (Oxford: Clarendon Press, 1968), 1058.

3. David Aune, *The New Testament in Its Literary Environment*, Library of Early Christianity 8 (Philadelphia: Westminster Press, 1987), 78.

4. Some manuscripts of the Septuagint place the break right after this notice instead, respecting its function as a macrostructural divider. See the textual notes in *Septuaginta* (Stuttgart: Deutsche Bibelgesellschaft, 1979) at 2 Sam. 24:24 and 1 Kings 2:11.

5. Analogously, some manuscripts of the Septuagint "stitch together" the separated parts of Samuel–Kings by repeating the opening words of one part at the end of the preceding one. This occurs in various manuscripts between 1 and 2 Samuel, 2 Samuel and 1 Kings, and 1 and 2 Kings. It also occurs at the break between 1 and 2 Chronicles.

6. Christopher R. Smith, "The Literary Structure of Leviticus," *Journal for the Study of the Old Testament* 70 (1996): 17–32.

7. Herbert Marks, "The Twelve Prophets," *The Literary Guide to the Bible*, ed. Robert Alter and Frank Kermode (Cambridge, MA: Harvard University Press, 1990), 208–9.

8. This fragment of the commentary is quoted in the *Philocalia*, chapter 3, "Why the Inspired Books are Twenty-two in Number," cited here in the translation by George Lewis (Edinburgh: T. & T. Clark, 1911), http://www.tertullian.org/fathers/origen_philocalia_02_text.htm#C3.

9. Origen's list is found in another fragment from the Commentary on the Psalms quoted by Eusebius, *Church History*, VI.25.2. A "Book

of the Twelve" is not actually listed, but can be inferred and is needed to arrive at a total of twenty-two.

10. *Philocalia*, chapter 3.

11. Kevin P. Edgecomb, trans., "Jerome's 'Helmeted Introduction' to Kings," http://www.bombaxo.com/blog/?p=218.

12. Ibid.

13. Roger Beckwith, *The Old Testament Canon of the New Testament Church and Its Background in Early Judaism* (Grand Rapids: Eerdmans, 1985), 502, n17.

14. G.C.D. Howley, "The Letters of Paul," *New International Bible Commentary* (Grand Rapids: Zondervan, 1979), 1095.

15. London: Geoffrey Bles and New York: Macmillan, 1963.

16. Beckwith, 181. It should be noted that Beckwith believes that the books of the Old Testament actually were in a fixed order in the time of Jesus. He thus considers the subsequent variations over the following centuries, in both Jewish and Christian versions of the Bible, a departure from this previously fixed order. Beckwith's overall goal is to establish that the *content* of the Old Testament canon was fixed by New Testament times. One argument he makes to this end is that the *order* of the canon was fixed by then. He supports this claim in various ways, but we do not need to consider his arguments here, since even if the Old Testament books were in a fixed order at the time of Jesus, Beckwith himself documents that their order became quite fluid right after the New Testament period. And it is precisely with the tradition that extends from after the New Testament period to the present that we are concerned. In terms of that tradition, a fixed book order truly is a "relatively modern phenomena."

17. Bruce Metzger, *The Canon of the New Testament: Its Origin, Development, and Significance* (New York: Oxford University Press, 1987), 295.

18. Kurt Aland and Barbara Aland, *The Text of the New Testament*, 2nd ed., trans. Erroll F. Rhodes (Grand Rapids: Eerdmans and Leiden: E.J. Brill, 1989), 79.

19. Metzger, 295–96.

20. Richmond Lattimore revived this presentation in our day in the first volume of his New Testament translation, *The Four Gospels and the Revelation* (New York: Farrar, Strauss, Giroux, 1979).

21. Metzger, 300.

22. Catholic Bibles additionally contain the deuterocanonical or apocryphal books, interspersed among the fully canonical books.

23. Mary Douglas carried this Hebrew convention over into English when she chose *In the Wilderness* as the title for her commentary on

the book of Numbers (Sheffield, England: Sheffield Academic Press, 1993).

24. Quoted by Eusebius, *Church History*, VI.25.2.

25. These names are attested by Philo and the Hellenist Ezekiel in Alexandria. Beckwith, 246.

26. Kevin P. Edgecomb, trans., "Jerome's 'Helmeted Introduction' to Kings," http://www.bombaxo.com/blog/?p=218 (emphasis added).

27. Lamentations may have been known by its first line because it was considered part of Jeremiah. In this case the first-line tradition gives an inaccurate indication of where a larger book boundary belongs.

Chapter Three

1. "The Structure of the Book of Revelation in Light of Apocalyptic Literary Conventions" *Novum Testamentum* 36 (1994): 373–93; "The Literary Structure of Leviticus," *Journal for the Study of the Old Testament* 70 (1996): 17–32; "Literary Evidences of a Fivefold Structure in the Gospel of Matthew," *New Testament Studies* 43 (1997): 540–51.

2. Richard Moulton, ed., *The Modern Reader's Bible* (New York: Macmillan, 1907); Ernest Sutherland Bates, ed., *The Bible Designed to Be Read as Living Literature* (New York: Simon and Schuster, 1936).

3. Robert Alter and Frank Kermode, eds, *The Literary Guide to the Bible* (Cambridge, MA: Harvard University Press, 1987); David E. Aune, *The New Testament in Its Literary Environment*, Library of Early Christianity 8 (Philadelphia: Westminster Press, 1987); Gordon D. Fee and Douglas Stuart, *How to Read the Bible Book by Book* (Grand Rapids: Zondervan, 2002).

4. *Christianity Today* August 9, 1999, 45–49.

5. *Books & Culture,* January/February 1998, 38–41.

6. Ibid., 40.

7. *The Twentieth Century New Testament* (London: Horace Marshall & Son and New York & Chicago: Fleming H. Revell, 1901).

8. Richmond Lattimore, *The New Testament* (New York: North Point Press, 1996). This volume combines Lattimore's *The Four Gospels and the Revelation* (New York: Farrar, Strauss, Giroux, 1979) and *Acts and Letters of the Apostles* (New York: Farrar, Strauss, Giroux, 1982).

9. Committee on Bible Translation, "A Word to the Reader," *The Holy Bible: Today's New International Version* (Colorado Springs: International Bible Society, 2005), v.

10. There were precedents for this approach in some earlier editions of the Scriptures. In *The New Testament in the Language of Today* (St. Louis: Concordia, 1964), William Beck used endnotes after each

book to document references to the Old Testament. In *The Modern Reader's Bible* (New York: Macmillan, 1907), Richard Moulton put all of the notes at the back of the volume. He placed no footnote indicators within the text, but instead used chapter and verse references and callout phrases within the notes themselves. For example, in the book of Ruth:

> **iii. 12.** *It is true that I am a near kinsman: howbeit there is a kinsman nearer than I.* The legal custom underlying the story seems to be an extension of what appears in the Mosaic law. . . . The story of Ruth implies that the obligation extended, failing a husband's brother, to whoever was nearest of kin (p. 1555).

11. The Bible Design Group, Preface, *The Books of The Bible: A Presentation of Today's New International Version* (Colorado Springs: International Bible Society, 2007), v.

12. *The Books of The Bible*, 1.

13. Ibid., 72.

14. Ibid.

15. There are other levels on which the Bible's inspiration is held to reside besides these two. An excellent discussion is found in Gabriel Fackre, *The Christian Story: A Pastoral Systematics, Volume 2, Authority: Scripture in the Church for the World* (Grand Rapids: Eerdmans, 1987), 60–91. Fackre documents further views such as, for example, those that the Bible is authoritative in that it is a witness to the "acts of God" in salvation history or because it is a means through which one may encounter Christ.

16. Similarly, at the end of each of the sections of the so-called "Book of Signs" in the first half of John, there is a reference to belief or unbelief in Jesus; at the end of the last section, John writes, "Even after Jesus had performed *so many signs* in their presence, they still would not believe in him," emphasis added.

17. The one other reference in the book to Jeremiah's words being written down comes at the start of the oracle about the new covenant, which has been given a central place in the collection.

18. Gordon Fee and Douglas Stuart, *How to Read the Bible Book by Book* (Grand Rapids: Zondervan, 2002), 333–39.

19. Aída Besançon Spencer and William David Spencer, Bible Study Commentary: 2 Corinthians (Grand Rapids: Lamplighter Books, 1989), 54–55. The Spencers actually divide their own book into chapters according to a topical outline, however, illustrating that interpretations of literary structure can be in conversation with one another even within the same commentary.

20. See Alexander Campbell, *The Sacred Writings of the Apostles and Evangelists of Jesus Christ, Commonly Styled the New Testament* (1826;

Nashville: Gospel Advocate Restoration Reprints, 2001), 57–105.

21. The Bible Design Group, Preface, *The Books of The Bible: A Presentation of Today's New International Version* (Colorado Springs: International Bible Society, 2007), vi.

Chapter Four

1. http://www.thebible.net/read/sched.html.

2. http://www.bible-reading.com/bible-plan.html.

3. Biblica has created some reading plans for *The Books of The Bible* that seek to be more respectful of natural literary units within the Scriptures. This particular discussion in Romans, for example, is assigned on a single day. http://thebooksofthebible.info/resources/readingplans.php.

4. http://www.ewordtoday.com/year.

5. http://www.ewordtoday.com/year/48/cjan01.htm (August 18–21 in the plan).

6. Sandra M. Schneiders, IHM, "Lectio Divina: Transformative Engagement with Scripture," *C21 Resources* (Boston College: The Church in the 21st Century Center), Spring 2009, 3.

7. N.T. Wright, *Following Jesus: Biblical Reflections on Discipleship* (Grand Rapids: Eerdmans, 1997), x–xi.

8. Donald Miller, *Searching For God Knows What* (Nashville: Thomas Nelson, 2004), 14.

9. See his extensive and very helpful discussion of the advent of writing and its effects on human culture and thought: Walter Ong, *Orality and Literacy: The Technologizing of the Word*, 2nd ed. (New York: Routledge, 2002).

10. Ong, 75.

11. And they still manage to be a pretty good read silently, as the best oral compositions can be. Readers of Lincoln's *Gettysburg Address* have tended to get much more out of it than the original hearers, who were barely seated when Lincoln began to speak and who considered him basically a warmup for the orator Edward Everett, who spoke that day at far greater length. Later readers, who are undistracted and have heard the verdict of history on the address, are actually in a better position to appreciate the eloquence of its language and the grandeur of its ideas. In the same way, the great biblical compositions, even though created and delivered orally, can hold their own against works that were written expressly for those with modern silent reading habits.

12. John H. Stek, "Psalm 103: Its Thematic Architecture," in J. Harold Ellens, ed., *Text and Community: Essays in Memory of Bruce M. Metzger*, vol. 1, New Testament Monographs 19 (Sheffield, England: Sheffield Phoenix, 2007), 23–38.

13. The divisions Prof. Stek identified are vv. 1–5, 6, 7–18, 19, 20–22. In Year A, verses 8–13 are read on Proper 19 (24), with 1–7 optional; in Year B, verses 1–13 and 22 are read on the Eighth Sunday after Epiphany and on Proper 3 (8); in Year C, verses 1–8 are read on Proper 16 (21) (http://lectionary.library.vanderbilt.edu).

Chapter Five
1. The Bible Design Group, Preface, *The Books of The Bible* (Colorado Springs: International Bible Society, 2007), v.

Chapter Six
1. This terminology is inspired by Gordon Fee and Douglas Stuart's book *How to Read the Bible For All Its Worth* (Grand Rapids: Zondervan, 1982). They write, for example, that "the task of interpreting involves the student/reader at two levels. First, one has to hear the Word they heard; he or she must try to understand what was said to them back *then and there*. Second, one must learn to hear that same Word in the *here and now*" (p. 20).
2. See the discussion in Stanley J. Grenz and John R. Franke, *Beyond Foundationalism: Shaping Theology in a Postmodern Context* (Louisville: Westminster John Knox Press, 2001), especially pp. 13–15 and 57–92. These authors describe the enterprise of modern biblical interpretation as that of identifying the "eternal system of timeless truths" that the "factual, propositional statements" in Scripture point to (pp. 13–14).
3. Dr. Fee may have put this in writing in one or more of his books, but I know the phrase from his recorded class lectures on various Pauline writings.
4. Pierre Grelot, *The Language of Symbolism: Biblical Theology, Semantics and Exegesis*, tr. Christopher R. Smith (Peabody, MA: Hendrickson, 2006), 103.
5. Brian McLaren, *The Story We Find Ourselves In: Further Adventures of a New Kind of Christian* (San Francisco: Jossey Bass, 2003), xi–xii.
6. Understanding the task of preaching, and more widely of biblical interpretation, to be that of situating our story within the larger story (following this apostolic model) helps to resolve part of what Peter Enns has identified as the "problem of the Old Testament." As Enns observes, "We, too, are living at the end of the story; we—as were the apostles—are engaged in the second, christotelic reading by virtue of our eschatological moment, the last days, the inauguration of the eschaton. As we read and interpret, we bring the death and resurrection of Christ to bear on the Old Testament." In other words, we are engaged in the definitive

retelling of the story, looking back over it from the privileged vantage point of the (beginning of its) end. Peter Enns, *Inspiration and Incarnation: Evangelicals and the Problem of the Old Testament* (Grand Rapids: Baker Academic, 2005), 159.

7. Grelot, 105.

8. Seeing the Bible as a *literary* whole in this way is not exactly the same thing as seeing it as a *theological* whole, although the two approaches are complementary. The latter approach has been described as a "theological reading" that looks for "the ways in which different parts come together to make a whole": "we read the texts in the light of their convergence in the pattern that centers on God's work in Jesus Christ and the subsequent sending of the Spirit." Stanley J. Grenz and John R. Franke, *Beyond Foundationalism: Shaping Theology in a Postmodern Context* (Louisville: Westminster John Knox, 2001), 90.

9. Richard B. Hays explores the richness of Paul's allusions to the First Testament, not merely in Romans but in all his letters, in *Echoes of Scripture in the Letters of Paul* (New Haven, CT: Yale University Press, 1989).

10. Glenn Paauw, "Organic Reference," *The Books of The Bible Blog*, February 5, 2008. http://blog.thebooksofthebible.info/2008/02/organic-references.php.

11. McLaren, *The Story We Find Ourselves In*, 75.

12. In the next chapter I'll share some further thoughts about this way of referencing within the Scriptures.

Chapter Seven

1. Daniel Haugh, "Shifting Our Physical Space In Youth Ministry," *Emerging Youth's Weblog*, Nov. 11, 2008. http://emergingyouth.wordpress.com/tag/solomons-porch.

2. Doug Pagitt, *Preaching Re-Imagined: The Role of the Sermon in Communities of Faith* (Grand Rapids: Zondervan, 2005).

3. Terry Dorsett, "Leading an Interactive Bible Study with Today's Teens," *Dr. T's Rambling Thoughts*, August 3, 2009. http://thoughtsfromdrt.blogspot.com/2009/08/leading-interactive-bible-study-with.html.

4. http://www.facingthechallenge.org/studyguide.pdf.

5. My translation. The phrase is in the genitive absolute.

6. In contexts like this, the Greek verb means to "hold a discussion." See *dialegomai* in BAGD (p. 185).

7. Steve Holmes, "Re-Imagining Preaching?" *Shored Fragments*, July 11, 2009. http://shoredfragments.wordpress.com/2009/07/11/reimagining-preaching.

8. This would address one of Pagitt's important concerns, which

is that, even in relatively smaller churches, people often hear "preaching from a stranger." They don't expect to develop much of a personal relationship with their pastor, and as a result, "the pastor remains a removed stranger who gives speeches about God." *Preaching Re-Imagined*, 88.

9. Quoted by Angus Kinnear in the preface to Watchman Nee, *What Shall This Man Do* (Fort Washington, PA: Christian Literature Crusade, 1973), viii.

10. The Bible Design Group, Preface, *The Books of The Bible: A Presentation of Today's New International Version* (Colorado Springs: International Bible Society, 2007), iv–v.

11. Christopher R. Smith, "Accommodate my Bible," *The Books of The Bible Blog*, April 22, 2008. http://blog.thebooksofthebible.info/2008/04/guest-blog-by-chris-smith.php.

12. Peter Enns, *Inspiration and Incarnation: Evangelicals and the Problem of the Old Testament* (Grand Rapids: Baker Academic, 2005), 162.

Conclusion

1. These frescoes were created from 1509 to 1512. Michelangelo later painted *The Last Judgment* on the altar wall of the chapel, and frescoes by other artists adorn the remaining walls, but I have chosen to use the ceiling paintings as an easily recognizable illustration.

2. Julie Ackerman Link, *Loving God with All My Heart* (Grand Rapids: Discovery House, 2004), 55.